S0-DUW-175

Selected Writings of John Finley Williamson

Compiled and Edited
By

Joseph G. Beck

Cover Photo by Orren Jack Turner

© 2004 by Joseph G. Beck. All rights reserved.

No part of this book may be reproduced, stored in a retrieval system, or
transmitted by any means, electronic, mechanical, photocopying, recording,
or otherwise, without written permission from the author.

First published by AuthorHouse 04/08/04

ISBN: 1-4140-3660-4 (e-book)
ISBN: 1-4184-0461-6 (Paperback)
ISBN: 1-4184-0459-4 (Dust jacket)

Library of Congress Control Number: 2003098486

This book is printed on acid free paper.

Printed in the United States of America
Bloomington, IN

Acknowledgments

The editor would like to express his deep appreciation to Ms. Heather Wessels for the layout of the manuscript and her insightful editorial assistance, the Reverend Thomas L. Dixon for providing copies of the out-of-print issues of *Etude: the Music Magazine*, Olin Library of Washington University in St. Louis, Otterbein College Library, and the Talbott Library of Westminster Choir College, Dr. Rhea B. Williamson for her speech at Otterbein College, and, of course, Dr. John Finley Williamson whose inspirational teaching has enriched all who knew him.

Joseph G. Beck, Ed. D.
St. Louis, MO 2003

Dedication

To my loving wife, Sara, whose inspiration
and devotion enriches my life daily.

Table of Contents

Foreword

John Finley Williamson founded the Westminster Choir in 1920 at the Westminster Presbyterian Church of Dayton, Ohio. Convinced that professionally trained musicians could best serve the church, he established the Westminster Choir School in September 1926 with sixty students and a faculty of ten. As the Choir School and its Choir's reputation grew, the demand for the School's graduates increased. The graduates came to be known as "Ministers of Music", a term coined by Dr. Williamson and still being used today by many church music programs.

As early as 1922, the Choir, then known as the Dayton Westminster Choir, began touring the United States annually and sang in such prominent places as Carnegie Hall (New York City), Symphony Hall (Boston), the Academy of Music (Philadelphia), Orchestra Hall (Chicago) and the White House for President Coolidge. Years later the Choir also sang for Presidents Roosevelt and Eisenhower.

The Westminster Choir made its first commercial recording with RCA Victor in 1926. Subsequently the Choir recorded with major conductors and orchestras; these recordings are listed in the Discography.

In 1928, the Westminster Choir and Cincinnati Orchestra conducted by Leopold Stokowski made the nation's first coast-to-coast radio broadcast on Cincinnati station WLW. A few years later because of the Choir's growing reputation it made a total of 60 half-hour broadcasts from NBC's New York facilities.

The first European tour took place in 1929 and was sponsored by Dayton philanthropist Katharine Hauk Talbott and endorsed by Walter Damrosch, conductor of the New York Symphony. The tour included 26 concerts in major cities of Europe.

Originally a three year program, the Choir School moved to Ithaca College in New York State in 1929 and enlarged its curriculum to a four year program culminating in a Bachelor of Music degree. This move ultimately proved unsatisfactory.

In 1932, the Choir School relocated to Princeton, New Jersey which became its permanent home. Classes were held in the First Presbyterian Church and the Princeton Seminary until 1934 when the Choir School moved into its present campus. This was made possible by a large gift from the philanthropist Sophia Strong Taylor. The dedication of the new campus was marked by a performance of Bach's Mass in B Minor at the Princeton University Chapel with the Westminster Choir, soloists, and the Philadelphia Orchestra conducted by Leopold Stokowski. Because of his high regard for the Choir, the services of the soloists, orchestra, and conductor were a gift from Maestro Stokowski.

There was a second European Choir tour in 1934 lasting nine weeks and highlighted by a live radio broadcast from Russia to the United States. It is interesting to note that in the fourteen short years since its founding in 1920, the Choir already had two European tours which earned it international acclaim and a campus of its own. The State of New Jersey in 1939 granted the Choir School accreditation and the name Westminster Choir College was adopted.

In years to come, under Dr. Williamson's leadership, the Choir would begin having regular concerts with the New York Philharmonic and the Philadelphia Orchestra. The Westminster Choir sang with the New York Philharmonic for the first time in 1939 conducted by Sir John Barbirolli. Since that time the Choir has sung over three hundred performances with the Philharmonic, a record number for a single choir to perform with an orchestra. Later that year the Choir sang with the NBC Orchestra conducted by Arturo Toscanini. That same year the Choir, directed by Dr. Williamson, sang at the dedication of the New York World's Fair which was broadcast to fifty-three countries.

In 1957, under the auspices of the U.S. State Department Cultural Exchange Program, the Choir undertook a five month world tour, concertizing in twenty-two countries, covering 40,000 miles and appearing before approximately a quarter of a million people.

Dr. Williamson retired as President of Westminster Choir College in 1958; however, he continued to give choral clinics and seminars around the world. Most notably in 1959, the U.S. State Department asked Dr. Williamson to organize a Westminster alumni choir to tour Africa. This choir was called the Westminster Singers. The African tour consisted of performances in fifty cities in twenty-six countries with audiences totaling more than 250,000. Following this tour, at the invitation of leading vocal teachers and choral conductors, Dr. Williamson's "retirement" consisted of conducting choral clinics and vocal festivals throughout the United States Japan, Korea and the Philippines. A South American choir tour was being planned by the State Department but was canceled because of Dr. Williamson's untimely death in 1964.

In accordance with his request, Dr. Williamson's ashes were scattered on the Quadrangle of his beloved campus on July 3, 1964. Dramatically this took place during the performance of the Verdi Requiem with the Westminster Festival Choir, soloists, and the Festival Orchestra conducted by Maestro Eugene Ormandy. This performance on the Westminster campus was part of the Tercentennial Celebration of the State of New Jersey. The following day a memorial service for Dr. Williamson was held in the the College Chapel.

The Etude articles included in this volume outline Dr. Williamson's vocal and choral concepts. The 1959 lectures are a further distillation and refinement of his philosophy. Also included is "A Singer's Guide to Diction in the English Language". The other items included are self-explanatory.

In 1976, the Choir College celebrated its fiftieth anniversary highlighted by a performance of Beethoven's Ninth Symphony with the Atlanta Symphony Orchestra conducted by Robert Shaw, alumni soloists, and the Westminster Alumni Choir on the Princeton University campus.

In 1996, Westminster merged with Rider University and is now known as Westminster Choir College of Rider University. The Choir College campus still remains in Princeton while the main Rider campus is in Lawrenceville, New Jersey.

In 2001, Westminster Choir College celebrated its seventy-fifth anniversary. For all those who love the choral arts, the accomplishments of Dr. Williamson are legendary. He was born in the nineteenth century, was a major influence and inspiration to the field of choral singing in the twentieth century; his influence and inspiration continues in the twenty-first century through the School he founded and its graduates. This is John Finley Williamson's lasting legacy.

Joseph G. Beck, Ed.D.

A Tribute to John Finley Williamson

by Bruno Walter

In 1942, I conducted Fidelio at the Metropolitan Opera, where I have since been active as guest conductor. Subsequent invitations from the splendid Philadelphia Orchestra have led to the formation of highly gratifying ties. Richly rewarding in both an artistic and a personal sense have been my occasional contacts with the Westminster Choir. When I think of America's musical culture and its future prospects, that choir, together with the accomplishments of the country's magnificent orchestras, inspires me with a sense of confidence. Raised and directed by the firm hand of Dr. John Finley Williamson, founder as well as head of the musical seminary whose pupils form the choir, it has succeeded by its vocal brilliance, its musicality, and its enthusiastic singing, in making a large number of oratorio performances deeply impressive. The secret of this impressiveness was revealed to me whenever I went for rehearsals to the university town of Princeton, almost English in its appearance. From the moment I was met at the station by Dr. Williamson till my departure I was gratifyingly conscious of the artistic idealism and cheerful faith emanating from him and inspiring his institution. I have never been able to work more easily, nor have I felt better understood than in the circle of these seriously enthusiastic youths.

—Selection from *Themes and Variations: An Autobiography by Bruno Walter*

The Secret of Training a Choir

by John Finley Williamson

The Christian Advocate circa 1920

The secret of training a choir is, of course, in giving the training dignity and worth. If choir members are allowed to come irregularly to rehearsals, and then allowed to slide through slipshod practices, and to sing publicly when they know that they are only half-trained, they will never regard the work of the choir with the seriousness it demands. The leader should never allow his choir to sing a number on which it is not fully prepared. Personally, I hold that full preparation means the ability to sing accurately and from memory. Nor should he allow laxness in attendance at rehearsals. In the Dayton choir, for example, two absences from rehearsals automatically vacate the place. But he should realize that this insistence on seriousness on the part of the singers calls for equal devotion on his own part.

By that I mean that every leader who asks volunteers to serve in a choir should give each volunteer at least one personal, private lesson a week as a reward for good work. You will find that such an arrangement as that will insure for a choir all the material it can desire. In our Dayton choir every singer is a volunteer, and we require four two-hour rehearsals a week. But, because we treat the subject honestly and because we give the individual singers training, as well as in the group, we have no difficulty in securing all the voices we could use.

Choir Organization and Training

by John Finley Williamson

Organ and Choral Conference, Music Teachers National Association, 1925

What we need for the present and future development of our church choirs is not organization. We need a realization and understanding of the part that the church can and will take in the musical development of our nation. Too long choirs have existed merely because custom demanded them and they have often been considered a necessary evil. They have rarely given artistic satisfaction and never that the spiritual stirring that the church has a right to demand from its music. This condition is almost entirely the fault of the church. Not knowing the power of music, not knowing the service that music can render to mankind, the church at large has ignored the whole subject. Each church in considering the subject usually thinks only of the selfish side. Each church tries to secure the most pleasing and most entertaining music,—music that will keep everyone in the church feeling good.

The church is slowly but surely awakening to a realization of its shortcomings in musical matters. The church of today is fast considering deeds as of more importance than creeds. She is asking how she may serve. The musician must answer in this case. The church has a power that the music educator dare not ignore. H.W. Krehbiel has said that only a singing nation can become a musical nation. We do not expect a nation of individual artists. If, however, our youths and adults can learn the joys of artistic choir singing we shall have made a great stride forward. Our oratorio and choral societies have waned, and justly so. Financial considerations seem to block most choral projects. The church can, will, and must finance a choral program for the nation. A real chance for service is there and the church is accepting the challenge.

Our public school musicians are working miracles with the children, but after high school most of our musical development stops for the lack of opportunity. The church must go hand in hand with the public schools in the musical development and musical education of the community. The church is finding a way to accomplish this. Four large denominations have appointed Commissions of Music. Spending as it does over a billion dollars a year on music the church is realizing that it secures no interest on its investment and even loses part of the principal each year. Such waste cannot continue. A program of education with service and worship must be substituted for the present hodgepodge.

How can this be done? First the church, concert-going and general public must be made to realize that choral singing is a high form of art. Second, we must find for our churches a plan that will coordinate a program of education for the individual, service to the community, and a program of worship for the church. For such a program I would suggest the following: that a department of music be formed in each church, this department to be formed under the control of one head and to include in each church a junior choir, ages 6-12, intermediate choir, ages 12-18, and an adult choir. In churches whose membership exceeds six hundred a high school choir, ages 16-21, should be organized and the adult choir start at the age of 21 instead of 18. Every church should have an orchestra. Each member of the adult choir should receive free voice lessons each week and the other choirs should receive regular group training. This program will take the entire time of one leader, a leader having the highest type of Christian character, sound musicianship, and a magnetic personality.

This whole plan stands or falls on the qualifications of its leadership. The church, however, is so much in earnest and is offering such fine salaries that within a few years some of our finest men will be found in this work. Then we may hope for the elimination of the cheap, sentimental, and sensational in church music, for a coordination of methods throughout all denominations, for the development of a tradition in choral singing, and for a unity of effort in each community that will make possible a choral program.

As to choir training I can only speak from my own experience, expressing my own views. Frankly, I am more interested in the training of choral conductors that choir singers. We have the above program in operation in Westminster Church. Realizing that our adult choir of the future must come form the high school, intermediate, and junior choirs we give greatest care to their training. However, the same general rules apply to all choirs. First, people do well only what they find joy in doing. Make your choirs love their work. The educational part must be given but it is best given sugar-coated. Let them sing. The wise director talks little. Second, people only find joy in honest intelligent work. The worst fault we have in choral music is the dishonesty shown in preparation. In the business and industrial world a man must do finished work to be even considered. In choral music we learn the notes fairly well, keep the time passably well, and then try to sing the number. This dishonesty takes the joy out of choir work. The singers soon lose interest and drop out. Hand in hand with the dishonesty in preparation is the lack of intelligent coordination shown in the building of our programs of worship. Sermons, hymns, anthems, scripture, prayers—all should have a definite relation. When they do not we subconsciously rebel. The choir should know the reason for each service and know why and how each hymn or anthem fits that service. When this is done and the number prepared so well that the singer may put something of himself in it he has experienced one of the great joys of life, the joy of honest, intelligent self-expression.

In the preparation of music certain things must be remembered. They are vitality in tone, naturalness in tone color, balance of parts, singing in tune, clearness of text, expression, rhythm, and sincerity. Vitality of tone in singing is the result of the exuberance of physical vitality. Too many of our choirs are flat-chested, hollow-eyed affairs. We must teach them the joy of vital bodies. Ruskin has said that architecture is frozen music. He could not have referred to most of our American choral music. A beautiful church will have a broad, deep foundation, with a towering, tapering steeple, while the choir in the same church will have four basses and twenty sopranos, throwing the whole structure out of proportion. The weakest point in our choral work in the balance of parts. Our second bass should be broad and heavy and the tone should taper through the other parts to a light, soaring first soprano.

When we have balance of parts we must face the question of singing in tune. If some of our tone structures could be frozen so that the conductor might analyze them he would be shocked. The best way to secure trueness of intonation is through a capella singing. Let a choir once experience the sheer joy that comes from being a part of a chord in tune with just or natural intervals and the battle is over. They will resent singing out of tune. It is a matter more of feeling than of hearing.

If a choir sings a well balance beautiful tone and no one understands what it is singing about, why sing? It is a shame the way we conductors dodge the subject. We print the text in our bulletins and on our programs and with this crutch we let our poor choirs sing on. It is most amusing to watch a group of people open their mouths, let sounds issue forth and not know the why of it all. There is no excuse for this. We must give time to the study of consonants, and this study coupled with a natural pure vowel will make us sing on our words. It will make us sing phrases and thoughts not sounds. We will then have accomplished one-half of the next point, expression.

Expression in choir work does not mean the sentimental dramatizing that so many vocal conductors attempt. An instrumentalist knows better. We must not forget that a choir is not a group of singers. It is an instrument. Its effects are instrumental. Its beauty of tone can rival that of the strings of our great orchestras while its power of dramatic utterance and spiritual appeal cannot be equaled. To secure these effects the conductor must have command of all vocal colors. He must have complete control of stress from pianissimo to fortissimo. Dramatic intensity must be a controlled power, not a wild emotional force. The choir must sing thoughts and not words and, too, the rhythm of the words must agree with the rhythm of the music. A chorus is not a percussion instrument even though many conductors try to make it one. Rhythm in choral work is a question of shadings and not of crude accents. Our church choirs are divided on this subject. They either over-accent, or, to give a refinement to their singing, they destroy all accent and make their tone structure a jelly-like mass. We must have accent, but the accent in choral singing is the bony skeleton that gives the form to our tone structure. We must cover the skeleton with lights and shades of tones that will make the whole structure glow and pulsate with life.

With all of this work we must have sincerity. We need not be hypocrites, but the man who does not have a religious impulse, a belief in God and a willingness to live in accord with his fellow men has no right in the choir loft. With sincerity his work will glow with a conviction that gives the final touch to artistry and our choir work will rightly take its place as an art work.

The Saga of the Westminster Choir

From a conference with
John Finley Williamson, Mus. Doc.
Founder, Conductor, and President
The Westminster Choir College, Princeton, N.J.

Secured expressly for the Etude by Andrew Martyn, August 1943

The saga of the Westminster Choir is now a part of American musical history. Dr. Williamson points out that while there have been innumerable newspaper and magazine critiques of the Choir's work, this conference is the first article of its kind to appear. Dr. Williamson was born at Canton, Ohio, in 1887. His father was a United Brethren clergyman. Dr. Williamson was graduated from Otterbein College of Westerville, Ohio. His interests primarily were in the development, beautification, and enrichment of the human voice. His objective was teaching and conducting singers, not singing. He concluded that the methods advocated by Francesco Lamperti and his son, Giovanni Battista Lamperti, stood at the forefront of the old Italian bel canto principles, and accordingly he studied for ten years under Lamperti exponents, Herbert Wilbur Green, David Bispham, and Herbert Witherspoon. For several years he taught voice and conducted the choir at the Westminster Presbyterian Church of Dayton. The success of the Choir was so notable that in 1922 it started upon tours to many eastern cities. In 1924 Mrs. H.E. Talbot, a wealthy patron of the arts, became sponsor for the Choir. Through her magnificent gifts, the Choir was enabled to make extensive tours in America; and in 1929 and 1934 tours, which created a furor, were made in Europe. The concerts in London, Paris, Berlin, Vienna, Prague, Leningrad, Moscow, Stockholm, Helsinki, Oslo, Copenhagen, and Amsterdam not only drew immense crowds and astonishing press criticisms, but also received recognition form the foreign governments, worthy of visiting diplomats. The Westminster Choir was the first foreign choral

11

organization ever to appear in Russia. At the Vienna State Opera it was the only organization, other than the State Opera, ever allowed to sing at the Opera House. At this performance the Choir received nineteen recalls at the end of the program. The group numbered sixty voices on its first tour and forty voices on the second. Mrs. Talbot at all times took an intimate, personal interest in the organization and accompanied it on tours. She was the sponsor of the Westminster Choir and, in the early days, made its touring possible. She thus gave the Choir, as a business investment, some $400,000, because she realized that she was assisting in providing America with what is now a "going concern" of great value in musical art. The Choir and the Choir College are now upon a self-supporting basis, insofar as current operating expenses are concerned.

In 1932 Dr. Williamson moved his activities to Princeton, New Jersey to be near the great cultural center, and particularly to have contact with the famous Princeton Theological Seminary. At Princeton, through a gift of Mrs. J. Livingstone Taylor, of Cleveland, Ohio, twenty-two acres and four splendid, modern Georgian Colonial buildings were secured, making an ideal background for the now-famous Westminster Choir College. The College has a faculty, in normal times, of thirty-two outstanding musicians and educators. There are thirteen pipe organs in the buildings. The teachers of organ are Dr. Alexander McCurdy, Dr. Walter Baker, David Hugh Jones, and Mary Taylor Krimmel. The Choir, during the past six years, has sung repeatedly under the batons of many of the greatest living conductors—Toscanini, Stokowski, Ormandy, Rodzinski, Bruno Walter, Barbirolli, Rachmaninoff, and others. Among the great master works presented repeatedly by these eminent musicians with the Choir are the Mozart "Requiem"; the Rossini "Petite Messe Solemnis"; the Beethoven "Ninth Symphony; the Rachmaninoff "Bells Symphony"; the Verdi "Requiem"; the Beethoven "Messe Solemnis"; the Bach "St. Matthew Passion"; the Mahler "Second Symphony"; parts of "Die Meistersinger" and "Parsifal"; the Berlioz "Romeo and Juliet"; the Berlioz "Damnation of Faust"; the Brahms "Requiem"; the Prokofieff "Andrew Nevsky"; and other outstanding works.

—Editor's Note—

****

It remained for Hector Berlioz in 1862 to make this pungent comment upon ordinary singers:

"A singer able to sing so much as sixteen measures of good music in a natural, well-poised and sympathetic voice, without effort, without affectation, without tricks, without exaggeration, without hiatuses, without hiccuping, without barking, without baaing—such a singer is a rare, a very rare, and excessively rare bird."

****

When the Westminster Choir College was started, it was realized that the most available form of human musical expression is the voice. While many play instruments, by far the greater number must depend upon singing. It seemed to me that the training of these people could best be accomplished normally through the churches, with choirs of singers of all ages.

In the earliest colonial days in America, singing was limited to the Psalms, and our forefathers were limited, in New England at least, to only five tunes which they droned over and over, Sunday after Sunday, as a religious duty; but certainly with very little musical joy. Gradually, as America developed, choirs came into existence. In many of these, there was very little contact with the spiritual purposes of the Church. In fact, the professional choirs which employed famous singers, in some instances but not all were anything but godly. Too often the old-fashioned organist of the Church looked upon his playing as the most important factor in the service. If he was a gifted player, he wanted the congregation to find it out every Sunday. He did not realize that, through his gifts and training as a choir director, he might produce the results which would enhance his position in the Church and in the community, as well as make closer bond between religion and music. When our work was first started we had considerable antagonism from organists of the old school, simply because they did not understand our purposes and were unwilling to investigate them. This, however, is now fortunately past, largely due to the indisputable recognition our artistic work has received.

The Choir College, when it started in 1925, was based upon the idea of training young musicians who not only would be good organists, good vocalists, and good conductors, but also would conscientiously take over the program of Christian education and young people's work as a part of the larger objectives of Church life. It is for this reason that so many of our graduates are known as Ministers of Music.

It has been my privilege and joy to work with hundreds of these young men and women, and the thing that has inspired me most is the sincerity and dignity with which they look upon their religious responsibilities, as well as their musical efficiency. After all, is not music in the Church, which is not carried along broad, tolerant lines of sincere devotion, little more than a poor travesty?

Sincerity and Dignity

Frequently we are asked to what we attribute the fame that the Westminster Choir has received. There is not secret about it. To me it is due to Divine guidance, to a wonderful faculty, and to a splendid wife, who never has missed a concert of the Westminster Choir, nor failed to give a subsequent merciless criticism of the work of the Choir after the concert. Mrs. Williamson has been Dean of the College since the beginning and is responsible for the course of study and for the curricula. Very fortunately she is gifted in doing things that I cannot do. For instance, we believe that the conductor must be not merely a musician, but must have the dramatic power of a great actor. Think of the famous conductors you know and you will realize how true this is. Our conductors' course is one of four years. Before the student approached the fourth year, he has had College English, Public Speaking, English Literature, and Drama. Why Drama in a college devoted to music—particularly the music of the Church? Mrs. Williamson, who conducts these drama courses, says: 'The ability to express the reality of mood through the spoken word, brings to the individual the emotional freedom through the spoken word that helps bring about perfection in coordination!' This is the great desideratum of the conductor! Accordingly, the student in the final years of his work must have taken part in the performance of at least ten plays.

There are those who ask why all of our students are required to study solfeggio after the manner taught in great European conservatories. The reason is thoroughness. It makes their subsequent work so much more definite and so much simpler. In the case of the Westminster Choir it was indispensable. All of the great conductors speak the language of solfeggio, and we could not accept engagements if our singers were not as familiar with it as with the alphabet. Nor could these young people ever aspire to be conductors of standing if they were unable to look at a score and hear it mentally. I feel that American musical education, in a bigger sense, will not get very far unless we employ the same technique which the masters and all the great orchestras have adopted.

Contact With Notables

One of our reasons for locating in Princeton, New Jersey, is that it is the center of a population of fourteen million people within a radius of fifty miles. This put us in easy contact with the great symphony orchestras, enabling our entire student body to work with these wonderful groups. Toscanini, for instance, has been on our campus five times this year, conducting rehearsals. In fact, many of the greatest living conductors have been in our College recently, giving the students first-hand, artistic training in studying masterpieces under foremost musicians. Every student in the school must play a keyboard instrument or an orchestral instrument. Our orchestra normally numbers sixty. Our Choir is just an average college group, known as a professional choir because they sing with these great orchestras. Every college group throughout the country can do the same thing, if they will affiliate themselves with the orchestras in their communities. It has been my ambition, however, to make the work of the Choir and the School of such a nature that all of our students will look upon it as a mission, rather than an obligation. It is hard to put this into words, but we realized that there were certain artistic values that money could not buy. It would be impossible for us to dream of securing, with a money consideration, the services of the internationally famous master conductors and musicians who have spent a great deal of time at the school rehearsing the immortal choral masterpieces for performances. Thus, our students are not merely studying in the usual manner of college students, but are making great music and presenting it under world-famous masters before a critical metropolitan public.

15

Joseph G. Beck

The American voice is now coming into its own, largely because our Americans are getting the results from superb training. Our public school system is marvelous. There is nothing like it in the world. The advance in the quality of voices during the past twenty years has been thrilling. The musicianship, the mental equipment, the physique, and the voice, because of proper training in the public schools, bring to us voices that are increasingly superior. Dorothy Maynor was graduated with us in 1936. Last year she was one of ten singers earning over $100,000.

Conductors often ask me what is the first thing I would recommend in taking up a new choir. Very well, I would insist first upon a good posture, standing or sitting. This should become an all-time habit; it greatly assists in bringing about correct breathing. For instance, I have seen choirs where the singers have been permitted to cross their knees. But this stiffens the diaphragm and inhibits correct breathing. The second step is the correct attack upon all vowels of the English language. Lamperti insisted that all vibration is in the voice box. The ordinary singer practices trying to say words, instead of trying to attack the vowel from the voice box. When my choir attacks a vowel on such a little phrase as this the sound is soft,

Ah

like a little grunt, but it is not really that. It is the elemental vibration of the vocal chords. It must be innately in perfect intonation and under full control to permit dynamic changes. The third step is the production of consonants, so that they are correctly articulated but never permitted to interfere with vowel production.

European Successes

The European trips of the Choir were an unceasing delight. Through the kind offices of President Hoover and President Roosevelt we had many wonderful introductions. Of course the Choir was, in a sense, in training, like a football team. We had regular rules conducive to health and rest, which were severe and could not be evaded. After all, the singer himself is his own musical instrument,

16

and these instruments were given as careful attention as a rare Stradivarius. Without this, the Choir tour could not have succeeded. But we had lots of fun and cultural advantages which the young people enjoyed hugely. Some very amusing incidents occurred. No member of the Choir forgot his vestment or his suitcase, but at one point the Conductor did forget. It was at our debut in England, in historic Bristol, whence came many of our pilgrim fathers to America. We arrived at the hall, and in the dressing room I found that I had left my dress trousers in London. The only thing I could do was to borrow a pair from an obliging usher. He wore my brown trousers all evening.

Music, at the time of our great national stress, is proving of immense value to the people. Our concert halls are thronged with vast crowds which obviously derive great relief and exaltation from the concerts. In the churches, music acts both as a consolation and as an inspiration. In camps here and overseas, it puts our boys in contact with the best. There is no morale builder to take its place."

****

All deep things are song. It seems somehow the very central essence of us, song; as if all the rest were but wrappages and hulls.
-Thomas Carlyle-

Joseph G. Beck

Introduction to Dr. Williamson's Articles

Etude Magazine, March 1950

Next month *Etude* has the honor of presenting the first in a series of articles by John Finley Williamson, founder and director of Westminster Choir College, Princeton, N.J.

Dean of U.S. choral conductors, Dr. Williamson also is a bold innovator who has been frequently at odds with traditional methods of vocal training. His unorthodox procedures, however, have achieved spectacular results with the Westminster Choir, Dr. Williamson's candid opinions about the state of U.S. singing today will interest all singers and choral conductors.

The new *Etude* series will constitute the first regular contributions by Dr. Williamson to any magazine.

The Art of Choral Conducting

by John Finley Williamson

Etude Magazine, April 1950

My first article for ETUDE readers cannot escape being nostalgic, because ETUDE had a profound effect on my own early musical development.

Because of Theodore Presser's interest in musicians in small communities, and in teachers, I discovered ETUDE. Through that discovery I met the three men who set the whole program for my life—Herbert Wilbur Green, David Bispham and Herbert Witherspoon.

My father was a minister. We lived in a small town, and Father's salary was meager. Being a builder of churches, and a generous man, he was always giving to others. There never was any money left over for buying music or taking music lessons.

For this reason, the hymn-book in the First United Brethren Church of Altoona, Pennsylvania, was my only textbook for piano practice—until I discovered the ETUDE. Even after 50 years I can still recall the excitement of first looking through its pages.

Theodore Presser's pioneering started my adventure in music. From that time on I learned each month to play the melodies and the chords in the music found between its covers. My first singing as my voice was changing was of songs found in the ETUDE.

Later I became interested in the vocal department of the magazine. The editor of the department at that time was Herbert Wilbur Green, one of America's great teachers. I even remember the article by him that first caught my attention. It contained a letter addressing this question to Mr. Green: "What can I do to eliminate the rasp in the male voices studying with me?"

Mr. Green's answer was, "For heavens sake, let the rasp alone. You women are always trying to take the vitality out of a man's voice."

This answer intrigued me, and I made it my business to get acquainted with Mr. Green. The result was that I studied with him over a period of five or six years.

I discovered that he was a pupil of the elder Lamperti. Inquiring after other pupils in the United States, I learned that David Bispham and Herbert Witherspoon were also students of Lamperti. I subsequently studied with them. The training with these three men laid the foundations for the vocal technique which I have used through the years with choirs and singers.

Thus in my own career I have been strongly indebted to the pioneer work of Theodore Presser. Filled with the spirit of adventure and with a strong creative bent, he built institutions that had an ideal of service. Coming from a small community himself, he knew the needs of individuals in villages and small towns.

Mr. Presser quickly discovered that too often music magazines served only musicians, so he sought to make ETUDE a publication that would help not only the teacher in the smaller community, but also the student, whose mind, filled with dreams, wonder and curiosity, was beginning its adventures in the realms of beauty through sound.

From the beginning he recognized that teachers, students and lovers of music had an interest in many varied forms of music. In his day the piano teacher was the outstanding musician in any community. Today the piano teacher still occupies an exalted place, but by his side are teachers from various fields of applied music—public school and church musicians, band, orchestra and choral conductors.

In almost any city or town, the last-named conductor is especially important. Undoubtedly the one phase of music which touches the greatest number of people is singing. Statisticians report that only 10 per cent of our population play any instrument. Thus, if the remaining nine-tenths are to have any creative expression in music, it must come through singing.

From the standpoint of sheer numbers, we have made a notable start toward becoming a singing nation. We have now in the United States a few great choirs. We have many good choirs, and we have thousands of choirs which are mediocre or less than that.

There are approximately 253,762 churches in the United States, having one to eight choirs each. There are 2,063 universities, colleges and junior colleges, in whose music education programs choirs occupy a very prominent place. In our 27,608 high schools, some of our best choirs are to be found. while in our public schools we find splendid choirs of treble voices throughout all the grades.

We may rejoice in the fact that we are earning the right to call ourselves a choral nation. Personally, my sincerest desire is to find a way to make the 90 per cent of our people who do not play instruments able to find new joy in creative expression through choral singing.

Materials are necessary for such a program. Since the war we have been developing the Westminster Choir College Library for the purpose of finding music for the touring Westminster Choir, of assisting college and high school choirs in their search for program material, and of satisfying the ever-increasing demand that continues to come from churches for music that lives and has a message for our day.

The Westminster Choir College, in conjunction with the Theodore Presser Company, will make this music known and available to all choirs and choir conductors who are interested in such materials.

This whole adventure is exciting to me. There is not only great music, composed in the past, which still lives today, but there is also great contemporary music. In addition to making this music available, we shall, through a series of recordings, present it as sung by the Westminster Choir, with accompanying teaching plans and instructions. Orchestral conductors have long used this method.

In these various ways I hope to present the fundamentals of good choral singing.

I have been privileged to work with many choirs. For 28 years I have toured with Westminster Choir throughout the United States, Canada and Europe, and through this touring I have discovered what kind of music gives the greatest joy to the choir member while he is singing and the greatest enjoyment to him in the future when his singing becomes a memory. I have also observed what kind of music creates in the audience an aesthetic appreciation that makes for lasting pleasure. During the past 14 or 15 years, Westminster Choir College has given about 115 concerts with the New York Philharmonic

Symphony, the Philadelphia Orchestra, and the NBC Symphony Orchestra, playing under some of the greatest conductors of our time.

In each of our performances under the baton of these inspired conductors, I have found certain fundamentals demanded.

Just what is meant by "fundamentals"? I shall be honored to present each month in ETUDE an article on choral singing. In future articles of this series I hope that I may be able to bring you an understanding of what I mean by the word "fundamentals". I shall endeavor to do this with sufficient clarity so that the solo singer, the choir singer and the conductor may gain something of value from the discussion.

Choral singing is complex, because it requires the doing at one and the same time of many simple things. A great choir is like a beautiful tapestry where single threads of silver and gold, of crimson and purple intertwine. The beauty of the tapestry depends not alone on the strength and beauty of the thread, but also on the artist, the skill and creative ability of the weaver.

Choir singing demands the same sort of weaving. You have the intertwining of threads of vibration that convey to the listener all colors, but this intertwining the choir singer rarely hears. His problem is the perfecting of his own thread of tone. For this reason we need a conductor who can hear as well as weave these threads in tone. If the weaving is done so that all these threads, each one beautiful in itself, intertwine and make patterns that unite the performer and the listener in aesthetic realization, great art has been achieved.

Balance the Voices

". . . a good choir should be a solidly constructed as a New England church."

by John Finley Williamson

Etude Magazine, May 1950

Glistening white spires, shining above green elms in a New England village, remind the approaching traveler that balance and proportion are an integral part of beauty. Balance is fundamental to beauty, to art, to life.

The artist, no matter what his medium—the dramatic or concert stage, painting or sculpture, poetry or preaching, instrumental or choral music—must accept and practice the principles of balance.

In our college and high school choirs, perfect balance is not always achieved, but its underlying principles are accepted. Efforts are made to achieve balance and proportion.

In church choirs such matters usually receive scant attention. In fact, one quickly gets the impression that it is more important not to hurt people's feelings than it is to be honest about any musical problem.

Recently, in one of our midwestern states, I was invited to give an address on choral music and conduct a demonstration choir clinic at a session of the State Music Teachers' Association. My clinic choir was on stage when I arrived. I checked numerical balance and found that I had 16 sopranos, nine altos, three tenors and one bass.

I asked the chairman why the group was so out of balance numerically. With a twinkle in his eye he answered: "This is what we put up with all year. We wanted to see what you would do with it."

I immediately had to bring the dynamics of all the voices down to where they balanced the single bass. The result was a good mixed quartet. After all, we were supposed to make music. Yet, oddly, some sopranos were offended.

One Sunday morning our family was on its way to Maine for a vacation. We stopped to attend church in one of those beautiful New

England churches which support those gleaming white spires. In the order of worship the bulletin listed a five-part anthem by Mendelssohn. When the choir stood up to sing we discovered there were nine women singing the soprano part, four or five the alto, and one lone man singing tenor or bass. To be sure, he was never heard, because, as in most church choirs, he was contending against an overpowering number of women's voices. The fifth, or solo part, was sung by the director of the choir herself, so the anthem, of necessity, developed into a contest between the director and the nine sopranos.

One other illustration: I was invited to conduct the Protestant choirs in one of our eastern cities. Since the choir numbered 3000 voices, it seemed wise that I hold a rehearsal with each section before the mass rehearsal. What was my amazement when I came to the soprano section, to find that, of 1100 women, only 65 acknowledged themselves to be lowly second sopranos. When I put a very large proportion of the remainder on the second soprano part, more than a few burst into tears.

Imagine a choir with 1000 first sopranos, and the other 2000 voices divided rather haphazardly among the second sopranos, first and second altos, first and second tenors, baritones and basses!

For some reason we have come to the conclusion that in our choirs we must have an overpowering number of sopranos. To be sure, Toscanini has said that the conductor's task is to keep the melody to the fore and to set the pace for the music; but keeping the melody to the fore is a matter of balance in stresses or control of softness and loudness, not of adding voices to the soprano section.

Chorus conductors must cease being afraid of hurting people's feelings. They must learn that having music that is beautiful in its balance and proportion is more important to the church than having most of the chairs in the choir loft filled with sopranos.

In all choirs the message that comes to the ear through the singing and the message that comes to the eye through a numerical balance should convey the same sense of balance and proportion that comes to us then we see those beautiful New England churches.

A ladder is useful in reaching high places, but no one risks his life on a ladder which has a narrow base and a wide top. For safety's sake, we want the base wide and the top narrow. For the choir's safety, the singing must be pleasing and secure through balance of tone.

A good choir should be as solidly constructed as the New England church. The first sopranos, with a simple and pure tone, may be compared to the glistening point of the spire. The second sopranos should be the base of the tower that supports the tapering top. The first and second altos, the first and second tenors and the baritones make up the body of the church. These singers should sing with tones as rich in color as old Cathedral glass. The structure must then be supported by the second bass.

A strong, firm foundation is essential in building a permanent structure. Therefore, the bass section is the basic element of the choir. The voices between the bass and first soprano impart rich tone colors to the ensemble, while the first soprano brings the whole structure to a focus through the shimmering clarity of a pure, crystal-clear thread of tone. Each section must recognize the importance of all other sections. A great choral ensemble cannot exist unless the soprano section will modulate its tone so that the bass can be heard. Thus, a good bass section can never take credit to itself, but must credit others who help build a balanced structure.

Likewise, a soprano voice that may be thin and lacking in overtone can be made to sound much richer than it really is through blending it harmonics with the harmonics of the low voices. The sopranos must then share honors with the bass and contralto voices. Realization of good balance is possible when each member of the choir works in conjunction with the others, as does a well-coordinated football team—each one coming to the fore when his section carries the melody, each one running interference for the section carrying the melody.

Often rewarding results come to the choir singer during rehearsal periods. Like a flash of lightning may come the realization that beauty is its own excuse for being. It may be the perfect tuning of a chord; it may be the realization on the part of the conductor and singer alike that tuning, timing and toning are instinctively or subconsciously achieved; or it may be the exhilarating assurance that through the vitality of their interpretation the listener has understood the music's inner meaning. And finally it may be that exaltation that each singer experiences when he knows that the spiritual values desired by the poet and composer have through his technique and mood been transferred to the listener.

Joseph G. Beck

Such rewards await the choral singer when he accepts individual responsibility in creating a beautiful tonal structure.

****

These, says Dr. Williamson, are the four fundamentals of choral singing:
1. Each singer must desire to help create a structure that is architecturally beautiful.
2. The acoustical laws of frequency in the creation of energy must be obeyed.
3. The acoustical laws of amplitude in the creation of energy must be obeyed.
4. Each individual whether in solo or choir work, must sing the part that allows him to do the majority of his singing in the middle of his vocal range.

Point 1 is discussed this month. Others will be considered in future articles in *Etude* by Dr. Williamson.

****

To the question of what should be "represented" in music, I venture in reply a paradox: Nothing, and everything. Nothing that is an imitation of outward perception, and everything that the artist has experienced as a result of outward perception. The man who imitates thunder in his music is merely displaying a bag of tricks; the man whose music makes me feel as if I had heard thunder is an artist.

-Goethe-

How to Classify Voices

Tenor or baritone, soprano or alto? The answer must be determined by more than range alone.

by John Finley Williamson

Etude Magazine, June 1950

Sometimes I think there is no subject more difficult for the teacher of singing and for the choir conductor than the classification of voices. In this article, we shall classify voices by quality, range and lift. Vocal quality and range are familiar aspects of singing. I believe, however, the lift is not as generally understood.

Before discussing the lift, let us reflect how voices are usually classified. Too many young people start singing the wrong part because their fathers or mothers sang that part before them and they wish to make the children over into vocal images of themselves. I remember the day when a father who had been a good singer brought his son to apply for entrance to our college. He told us that the son must sing tenor because that was the part both he and his father had sung. The son was well on the road to completing his medical training and did not want to go to a school of music. Above all else he did not want to become a tenor because his voice was certainly baritone. The only possible decision was that he return to medical school.

False idealization so often influences young singers. We are all deeply moved when we hear some great artist. But the young singer, after such an experience, decided that he wants to sing exactly like that artist. He attempts to sing the same part and tries to model his voice for the phonograph records of that artist. An imitation is always an imitation. Since we cannot hear our own voices, we must be willing to trust the judgment of those who can hear with discriminating ears. Such persons classify voices by the quality of the voice, by the range of the voice and by what the old Italian masters called "registers" or "breaks."

Joseph G. Beck

Some voices can be immediately classified by their quality or timbre. Such are the exceptions, however. Most of us are not so fortunate and must work to achieve naturalness in our voices.

Many women who think they are sopranos are certain they are first sopranos. In one day I heard over 300 young singers from one state who were members of their all-state choir. I took a day to make sure each singer was singing the right part. I heard one beautiful young voice trying to sing first soprano when she had a glorious dramatic soprano voice, but of course it had not yet matured. I placed her in the first alto part. That afternoon both the father and mother were waiting to see me. "My daughter has a 'coloratura' voice. You must put her in the first soprano section, because that is the best section."

Coloratura voices are as rare as first sopranos. The truth is that sopranos wish to sing first soprano either because they cannot read music, or because vanity makes them feel that the word first is more important than the word second. Personally I believe that the soprano sections of our American choirs produce the most unpleasant sounds and are usually the weakest sections.

Basses and contraltos also try to change the timbre of their voices so that they may be impressive with their bass and contralto quality. The result is in almost all cases a sad, lugubrious quality that keeps these sections almost always out of tune. The tenor has his own vanity, and so he tries to sing with what may be termed a "necktie" quality, singing as if someone were trying to choke him to death with his necktie.

The quality the average choir singer uses can give us much insight as to the correct classification of his voice. The recognition of quality is part of voice classification but not the whole.

Using range alone to classify voices is also dangerous. A pure coloratura voice will often have good low tones. If in her early youth the coloratura has been able to read music well, she is too often placed in the alto section. Likewise a pure contralto voice will also have a good high voice, but if she can't read music she will in probability be found in the first soprano section.

It is a well-known fact that the great tenor Caruso and the great baritone Scotti had almost identical ranges. Caruso's low F was as good as Scotti's low F. Scotti's high C was as good as Caruso's high

28

C. Night after night these two great artists sang together in the Metropolitan Opera House, each one singing the majority of the time in the part that was for him the most comfortable range of his voice.

They knew they were right. They knew where their lifts were— not because of the range of their voices. Knowing the range helps, but it is not the final consideration. We can only classify voices accurately, (1) when we decide whether the quality is absolutely natural, or affected; (2) when we concede that the range in most voices is rather wide and does not tell us too much about classification; and (3) when we learn to recognize the lift in the voice.

Herbert Witherspoon, a student of the elder Lamperti, graduated from Yale University, having had there a particular interest in psychology. When he finished college he found his real place in life in singing. He became one of the Metropolitan's great bassos and later the General Manager of the Metropolitan Opera Company. When he started teaching singing his studies in psychology convinced him that the words "register" and "break" were not constructively correct. So it was he who first used the word "lift." He used this word because he felt that it most adequately described what should happen in the individual's thinking at the place in the voice where the break or change in register seemed to be. He first advanced the idea that the use of the knowledge of lifts with the knowledge of quality and the knowledge of range of the individual voice gave absolute certainty in classifying the individual voice.

The lift is a place in the range of the voice where it is necessary to use less breath. The lift is the place where the voice becomes easier to produce, and where the singer senses a spontaneous buoyancy in ascending scales. At this place the singer can find correct and natural pronunciation through his own mental activity. The realization that the lift exists helps the singer to know that tones that are mistakenly called high tones are more easily produced than the so-called low tones.

The study of acoustics proves to us that fast vibrations are created with less effort than slow vibrations. The keys in the treble part of the piano require less pressure to produce the sound from the strings than do the keys in the lower or bass part of the piano. The violinist uses less physical activity in playing than does a double bass player. The same is true in singing. The coloratura soprano uses much less

29

physical strength when singing than does the basso profundo. In over 28 years of touring with the Westminster Choir, rarely have any of my first sopranos fainted, but I always have to watch my second basses. This seems strange when one realizes that great basses are usually giants and coloratura sopranos are usually on the petite side—for example, Lily Pons.

When we study acoustics we accept the law that fast vibrations are easier to produce than slow vibrations. If we accept this law we must accept the conclusion that so-called high tones in the singing voice are easier to produce than the so-called low tones.

When the average singer sings what he calls a high tone he "reaches" for it, either sharping the pitch or never attaining it at all. The same type of singer in singing the low tones tries to depress his whole vocal mechanism to produce this low tone and usually flats the pitch.

The musical notation that has come to us through the centuries is for the eye and must be retranslated for the ear if we are to make music. The symbol of a quarter note on the first line above the staff is called "high A." In reality this symbol must be translated to the listener through a vibration which comes to him through the air at a rate of 880 vibrations per second. When this note is played by the pianist he never reaches up above the piano to play it. The whole scale is one level. The same should be true with the human voice. The scale is in the voice box. When a singer sings the note on the second line below the staff he is not singing a tone that is low, but a vibration that is slower than the A on the first line above the staff. The tone on the second line below the staff has only 220 vibrations per second. Therefore, because it is so much slower it is harder to produce.

If the singer and conductor can accept the fact that music is horizontal flow, not vertical flow, they will quickly find tensions leaving the singer's throat, developing a new coordination between his body and the voice that he gives forth. To achieve this coordination it is absolutely essential that the singer and conductor understand lifts. The understanding of lifts makes the whole problem of voice much simpler. It means that on the note where the lift occurs the singer must use a modified pronunciation that will in turn require much less mental pressure. Because less mental pressure is used, less breath will be used, less oxygen will be used, vocal tensions will leave and fear of high tones will disappear. With the loss of fear in producing so-called high tones the singer will suddenly find that he has new freedom in producing his low voice.

Young people possess so much physical exuberance that often they enjoy these muscular tensions which cause the local effort in the muscles around the vocal cords. Such individuals should run two or three miles or play a couple of sets of tennis before they take their voice lesson or come to choir rehearsal. Singing necessarily demands a powerful body, but the application of power is not directly through the muscles. It is applied through the mind. The individual who gets his joy from muscular tension and physical distortion will perhaps not enjoy singing when he first finds that the realm of vocal art uses the body only as an instrument, controlled by the mind and, we hope, by a strong imagination and a deep spiritual understanding. When a voice is classified correctly and obeys the laws that are centered around the lifts, artistry begins to develop. The singer makes the wonderful discovery that art in singing is based upon the creation of a beautiful line. He will also quickly learn that good ensemble work depends on balance and proportion in the weaving together of these lines. His creative powers will suddenly begin to unfold and new experiences in the whole realm of living will be his.

Make Friends with Acoustics
Several basic laws of engineering can make or break fine choral tone.

by John Finley Williamson

Etude Magazine, November 1950

At this time of year, church choirs, high school choirs, college choirs, community choirs, and professional choirs all begin a new season's activities. Some will have a gloriously exciting year from start to finish; others will tolerate their conductor and others will be tolerated by their conductor. Some choirs will stay together throughout the whole year because of the delightful social times they will experience; other will stay together from a sense of duty. I hope that many will experience the excitement that comes from recreating the beauty created by the masters, will bring exhilaration, hope and beauty to those who hear them sing.

When the choir experience is an exciting one for its conductor and its members it is partly because the sections are well balanced and the architectural structure of the whole is a thing of beauty. Such an experience can result when the individual voices have been classified correctly and when the conductor and singers have obeyed at all times the laws of acoustics concerning frequency and amplitude.

In studying the laws of acoustics, we find that when frequency doubles, energy squares. The doubling of frequency produces a tone one octave higher. Thus, when a soprano is singing three octaves above a bass, the energy produced in her voice is many times that of the bass, since frequency has been doubled three times and energy squared each time.

This suggests why men dislike to sing when the soprano tone is big and overpowering. Men lose interest when they can't be heard. This may explain why you often find choirs with 16 or 17 women singing soprano and one poor man singing bass. No doubt long ago the other men lost hope of ever being heard. Great choirs will always have more basses then they have first sopranos and they will use only

33

the light voices on first soprano. If you wish to have a good male section in your choir, make sure that your women are balanced with light voices on top and heavy voices on bottom. Such an arrangement makes it possible for the men always to hear the male tone. Even though you may be rehearsing in a small room where the women's voices tend to be lost, be assured that the instant you sing in a large auditorium, because of the law of frequency, the women's voices will always be heard above those of the men.

In developing the melodic line in all parts, this law must be obeyed. The tendency on the part of every voice is to increase the volume of the tone when an interval moves up such as a third, fifth, sixth, or octave. No increase of volume in tone should be allowed the soprano part in an upward ascending interval unless the increase is called for in all parts. In almost all cases you will find that the volume of the tone in the soprano part must be decreased when the melody moves up if you wish to keep the volume of the overall tone on an even level. Since the soprano section has at all times the advantage of frequency in creating energy, the entire section should carefully watch that all ascending intervals are kept in the dynamic balance of the phrase line.

In the hymn, "Fairest Lord Jesus," the soprano in the words "Fairest Lord Jesus" sings the first phrase beginning with the keynote, F. They start the second phrase, "Ruler of all nature," on the third, A. The words of the third phrase, "O Thou of God and man the Son," begin on C and leap to an F on "Thou." Invariably in choirs and congregations the women's voices slide from the C to the F with a great crescendo drowning out everything else. Rather, the three phrases should be sung starting the words "Fairest Lord Jesus" on the F with a natural volume of voice, the second phrase, "Ruler of all nature" with somewhat less volume, the word "O" on the C with less volume, and the F with still less volume. If this plan of balance is carried out correctly, the tone on the F above will seem no louder than the tone F an octave below on which it started, and all other parts will be heard because they have been equally balance with the sopranos.

The second acoustical law, "when amplitude doubles, energy squares," will be followed also. If the outside parts of the chord are three octaves apart, the soprano tone or top of the chord creates 12 times the energy that the bass tone or the bottom of the chord creates.

34

To achieve a more equal balance, in the Westminster Choir we try to do as follows:

The first soprano, made up of five voices, is divided. The two in the E lift sing the top of the chord, the three in the E-flat lift sing the second soprano part. The five second soprano voices then go to the first alto and the five first alto voices join the second alto, giving a numerical balance of two first, three second, five first alto, and 11 second alto. In our male voices, the heaviest first tenor joins the second tenor; the two heaviest second tenors join the baritone; and the two heaviest baritones join the bass giving a numerical balance of three first tenors, three second tenors, five baritones, and eight second basses. This method which allows eight second basses on the bottom of the chord is particularly advantageous on wide-spread chords. If there is still too much first soprano tone, we increase the amplitude of the second basses in their tone so they balance the energy created by the first sopranos.

We find it much easier to keep the choir in tune if the basses increase amplitude when they sing the low tones, and the sopranos decrease amplitude as they ascend.

If the choir is in balance the conductor can readily weave the tapestry of tone so that every part can be clearly and distinctly heard no matter how low or how high other parts may be singing. The result is that each section in the choir feels equally important and each member in each section feels equally important because out of correct balance comes symmetry and proportion to all parts of the tonal structure.

Keep Your Choir Up to Pitch

Singing in tune is the result of knowing and obeying fundamental laws of sound

by John Finley Williamson

Etude Magazine, December 1950

The first problem a choirmaster faces with a new choir is that of singing in tune. When an individual or a choir does not sing in tune, there is no music.

Singing in tune is the result of knowing and obeying certain fundamental laws. Music is not an accident. Our musical scale, with its intervals and then its chords, came into being as a result of man's continual search for beauty through the centuries. With our acceptance of a scale, we must also accept the relation of one tone to another in the scale. This relation is not haphazard; it follows strict mathematical principles first formulated by Pythagorus more than 2,000 years ago.

Knowing the rules for singing in tune, the singer then must have sufficient technical skill to put them into practice.

Singing requires energy; hence to sing in tune an individual must first have an abundant supply of oxygen in his bloodstream. From touring, we of Westminster Choir early discovered that we had to be concerned with ventilation in the auditorium in which we were singing. If our singing brought pleasure to the audience, the problem of ventilation increased. Therefore we were much more likely to fall in pitch.

In motion picture theaters it has been discovered that when a dramatic picture is shown the air conditioning system will often break down, whereas a quiet pastoral picture will not affect the air conditioning in the least. This is due to the fact that when an individual uses his emotions he uses up more oxygen. Similarly, we have found that a pleasing program arouses emotional excitement in the individual, and because of this he takes more oxygen out of the air in the auditorium.

Today we know that the instant our eyes burn in the slightest, we must watch for tightening in that little muscle in the back of the head, situated at the base of the brain, called the medulla. When that tightens, there is a definite oxygen shortage in the air, and the choir will immediately start flatting. Nothing the conductor can do will hold them to pitch until the oxygen shortage is made up in each singer's bloodstream.

The conductor also must be careful about the circulation of fresh air in the rehearsal room. An abundant supply of oxygen will keep each singer wide awake and keep his voice in tune.

The second requirement for singing in tune is correct posture. In many choir rehearsals, particularly church choirs, the thinking appears to be that if the singer gives his time and his voice to the Lord, he should not be called on to give his physical vitality and mental activity. So, in rehearsals, the singers drop one arm over the back of the chair, slump down until they are sitting on their shoulder-blades, cross their knees and defy God and man to do anything about it.

The singer should stand with the arches of his feet raised to a position of activity, as if he were shadow boxing. The pelvis should be straightened, as a result of which the abdomen is lifted and held in position by the muscular activity in the abdominal wall. The shoulders are brought forward and down to a position which in turn spreads the back ribs, and the head then rests straight on the spine. A plumb line dropped from the ear should go down through the shoulder, through the leg and come out through the arch in the foot. This is the posture of youth, of vitality, of physical health, and it obeys the laws of beauty that we admire. As soon as this natural and vital posture is achieved a great many of our problems of pitch and tuning are solved. When we have adequate oxygen supply, when we achieve natural balance in posture we are then ready to study the question of pitch in singing.

The ability to sing intervals in tune is the result of memory. Any individual who has a good memory and can recognize an interval can easily sing it correctly. I am told that formerly the majority of the children in Budapest had absolute pitch. This was due to the fact that they recognized in the public schools that pitch was a matter of memory. Hubay, the great Hungarian violinist, was responsible for this.

One night in Geneva, Switzerland, we were guests in the home of a prominent world churchman. Westminster Choir had sung the night before in Geneva's beautiful concert hall. Three children were seated at the table with us. Suddenly the children could be contained no longer. They wished to ask questions. The first question was to what pitch should the piano be tuned. When I answered A-440 a shout of glee went up. The father, a world churchman, did not understand how important pitch could be to children. Upon inquiry the next day I discovered that the majority of children in Geneva had absolute pitch. This came about because Jaques Dalcroze, the great music educator of Switzerland, was in charge of the music in public schools, and recognized that pitch had a great deal to do with memory.

Parents all should know this principle. If the fixed sounds about the home can always sound at A-440, if the little children can always hear their songs sung in the same key—this should start when they are two—suddenly the parents will realize that the children thereafter will always sing the songs in that key and the beginning of a good pitch memory has been established.

To make this principle apply to choir work the conductor should at the first rehearsal start tuning the sections in four- or eight-part chords. The chords should never be played at the organ or piano. The conductor instead should obtain a small ten-inch Deagan chime, tuned at A-440. Its vibrations are guaranteed. That is seldom true of church pianos and organs, and sometimes not true of school pianos. The chime has the advantage in that the sound continues for quite a few seconds after that pitch has been sounded. First, sopranos should sing the same pitch, and the conductor should insist that every voice in that section tune until the unison pitch in all voices is A-440. Then the second bass should sing the A two octaves below, again continuing to tune until each voice in the section can match pitch. The first tenors and second altos should sing the octave between the bass and sopranos, or A-220, again each section tuning its unison A. When the three pitches are tuned in each section then the two octaves should be tuned together with the Deagan chime sounded frequently so that the original pitch stays in the memory. As soon as the octaves are in tune the second sopranos and second tenors should be taught to tune the fifth, which is E, each section working alone until the unison of the section is in accord. When the six sections are able to sing the octaves and fifths in tune then the first altos and baritones should tune the third, C-sharp. When the unison of each voice is in accord the entire chord of two octaves may be sung, while still sounding the Deagan chime of A.

In the tempered scale that is used in our pianos and organs the thirds are sharped and the fifths are flatted. In the untempered scale of Pythagorus the opposite is true. The conductor will find that in unaccompanied singing the choir will gradually sing the third a little lower and raise the fifth a little higher. As soon as the choir is able to sing an interval of a fifth in untempered tuning, they will be delighted when they hear for the first time the harmonic that results.

A great string quartet that practices four hours a day spends 40 to 50 minutes of that time in tuning. A choir that practices two hours a week should spend at least 15 minutes out of the two hours in learning to sing chords with perfect untempered intonation.

At first the chimes should be sounded frequently. Later on, the chime will not be needed except for the initial sounding of pitch. The choir is beginning to remember A.

If possible, it is wise to purchase an A and a C chime. As soon as the choir remembers A it is good then to move the chord up to C.

We in Westminster Choir tune to a G, A, C, and D. In that way we solve all of the problems of lifts. If the voices in the choir have been classified according to lifts, tuning to a G chord will put every voice in its chest or lowest position except the first sopranos, who are in the middle voice. A chord on C will put all the women in middle voice, leaving all the men in chest voice. The D chord keeps all the women in the middle and the first tenors in the first lift. If the choir is small and wishes to tune to a four-part chord the bass should sing A-110, soprano A-440, the tenor the fifth above the bass, or E, and the alto the third or C-sharp below the A of the soprano.

Knowing that pitch has to do with memory can also help greatly in sight-reading with the choir. The average individual is not a good sight-reader because he has not memorized all the intervals.

When the choir is sight-reading and one section sings a wrong interval, the conductor should immediately sing the melody of some popular song or hymn in which the first interval is the same interval that caused the mistake.

The hymn "Holy, Holy, Holy," sung to the tune "Nicea," has a third as the first interval in the melody. The first interval in "Hark, the Herald Angels Sing" is a fourth. The first interval in "God Rest You Merry, Gentlemen" is a fifth. The first interval in "Who Is on the Lord's Side" is a sixth. These are suggestions taken at random from the Presbyterian Hymnal. We advise each conductor to use the hymnbook of his church for his melodic material in intervals.

When singers in a choir realize that they know all intervals, it will be an easy task for them to learn to recognize these intervals when they appear in music that is not familiar. By using the same melodic material all the time, each individual in the group will have his intervals memorized and sight reading will improve.

Nothing in sound can be any more beautiful than a major triad on C with a third and fifth tuned to the untempered scale. Then this chord is perfectly tuned, harmonics are sounded and the voices are richer than they have ever been before. A beautiful red rose is to me a chord in C Major, since the vibration of the color red is 32 octaves above middle C. When a choir learns the art of singing in tune and obeys the laws of pitch, new joy comes to them and to the listener. The vibrations of the music created by such a choir find response in the whole being of the listener, and a feeling of oneness comes over singers and audience as they realize that all tune to a spiritual unity.

Rhythm Makes the Music Go
Keeping time in choral singing is more complex than merely counting four in a bar.

by John Finley Williamson

Etude Magazine, January 1951

The most difficult task a choir master faces is that of making his choir sing in correct time and yet keep the music moving forward in rhythm. Peculiarly it seems more difficult for a choir to master correct time values than it does for it to master correct pitches.

Early in childhood we learn to count. There is not an individual in any part of the United States who does not know that two and two make four, that one and a half and a half make two, that four ones make four, but the instant dotted notes, eighth notes, sixteenth notes, thirty-second notes and triplets appear the individual's mind becomes confused and he starts singing them to the wrong time.

Personally I believe our trouble has come from the fact that our study of time in music has been on a wrong basis. We are early taught to count time with regular accent, perhaps because the dictionary defines rhythm as "regular recurring accent." We are prone to believe that all accents are developed through time values. However, a change in pitch, a new chord, or timbre creates an accent. By changes in timbre I mean changing from soprano to alto, or to tenor, or to bass. All of these forms of accent are determined by the composer, who must have created them as he wished them to be, and certainly they should be recreated by the performer, whether he be singer or conductor, without the addition of falsely accentuated time values.

I have found that if I think of time values as pitch duration's only, my choir has a much simpler time in phrasing and in keeping a legato line. So many of us in church music try to keep a regularly recurring accent such as **1** 2 **3** 4 **1** 2 **3** 4. This seems to make the singing of choral music easy, but in reality it makes it cease to be music. How can one crescendo unless the accents are increasing in volume, or how can one decrescendo unless the accents are decreasing in volume?

43

If we can accept the idea that time is merely the duration given to each pitch, we shall lose all desire to give false accent to these pitch duration's. And the natural accents created by the composer, through changes in pitch, changes in pitch duration, changes in chord, will be heard without offending the listener with false time accents.

With this concept in mind, time values are easily taught to a group. They are easily taught because we recognize that time in music is not a mental thing but a forward-moving rhythmic progression of pitch duration's. The deadening result of choral music when every individual counts and keeps "perfect" time without a through of rhythm is the thing that makes choral music more objectionable than anything else, whereas if the music be made to move forward, it becomes a living pulsating thing, which brings joy or sorrow, gladness or pain to the listener.

Who doesn't enjoy the ballet and who doesn't enjoy tap dancing? The Rockettes at Radio City Music Hall are an excellent example of living rhythm. Choral music can be just as alive as tap dancing, ballet or the Rockettes, but no satisfactory result can be achieved if the group is allowed to count time or even think the time value given to each note.

There is a positive way that correct pitch duration's can be achieved in a forward-moving rhythmic progression. If each number that the choir sings is clapped out by the hands before the choir even attempts to sing it, a rhythm sense will be developed very quickly. This clapping should not be dainty, easy tapping, rather the tips of the fingers should strike the palm of the hand with vigor and strength, so that each note in the music is represented by a sharp vigorous clap. Bach becomes a beautiful experience in timing when such a method is used. The performance of Mozart, Haydn and Handel can be made extremely simple when the rhythm is thus established. Each individual becomes conscious of a muscular sense of a forward moving progression which is so essential in music. May I repeat again that the tapping must be firm and vigorous so that it almost stings the hand. Timing must be translated through the muscular reaction in the body.

After the tapping is correct throughout an entire number, it is wise to sing and at the same time continue the tapping. Here the conductor will face a definite problem. Individuals can tap in rhythm, they can

44

march and dance in rhythm but they will not sing in rhythm without much prodding. If they sing in rhythm they must think, and people generally prefer not to think. The vague non-rhythmic wandering that most choirs go through allows the individual singer to interpret individual words with no thought of the line or rhythmic pattern created by the composer. It also allows him to close his eyes, shake his head from side to side and use all the bad mannerisms that singers who cannot sing always use. If the conductor demands that the song be rhythmic the singer must think and understand the interpretation of his song. He must know what the music says, and he must so control amplitude as to make the rhythmic progression set forth a pattern that expresses what the composer felt when he created the music.

The conductor will find a new joy in his conducting. Suddenly his beat seems to spring along because the choir is not everlastingly dragging out each time value. The conductor will find that the choir need not watch him so closely as he thought necessary, nor remember his series of do's and don'ts, for suddenly all rhythm is translated through their bodies and a unity and a oneness of expression, not to be compared with the deadening monotony of counting **1** 2 **3** 4, is achieved. The leader will also find that he is ceasing to be a time beater, and beginning to be a conductor.

I can't urge too strongly that the leader require every individual to tap the rhythms vigorously. Lazy and non-rhythmic members will still be lazy and non-rhythmic if they are not forced to use vigor. If they will not cooperate, they should be asked to resign from the choir.

This same plan should be followed in revitalizing our hymn singing. If the choir and organist can get away from the percussion effects that are so often used in congregational singing and come to the rhythmic legato effect produced by good string players, hymn singing will again take its place as one of the beautiful experiences in worship.

Tuning seems difficult—in fact well nigh impossible—to most choirs, but if a pitch memory is developed in the choir and the practice of tapping in timing is carried on actively, tuning suddenly improves. It is the non-rhythmic individual who usually is the poorest in tuning. When each member in a group becomes rhythmic, good tuning seems to be the natural result.

Joseph G. Beck

This type of timing is also very beneficial to singers as individuals. We have through the years so developed our pet ways of getting attention that it is difficult for us to be a part of a group. We rather prefer to be little dictators in our own realms. As soon as we accept the joys of rhythmic progression in music, we accept one of the greatest privileges of democracy, that of working with and going along with others in rhythmic control. If this plan is carried on consistently through rehearsal after rehearsal, problems of discipline will iron out, because each individual will find the joy of creating a line in music that is in tune, and, above everything else, is in rhythm. When that joy is found one tends to forget self.

Westminster Choir has been privileged to work with almost all of the great conductors, having had many performances with each one of them. We have found that these great conductors may forgive a wrong pitch, but they will never forgive bad rhythm. Bad rhythm means chaos, and if the faulty rhythms are allowed to continue the performance is certain to disintegrate. The best advice that can be given to a singer whether he be a soloist or a member of a choir is to learn to sing in rhythm. In order to do this the singer must not think of time as an accent but of time as pitch duration's that are always moving forward in a phrase pattern which carries the inner meaning of the music to the listener.

Correct Breathing for Singers
Despite the elaborate theories advanced by many people, no thinking and no muscular control are required for breathing.

by John Finley Williamson

Etude Magazine, February 1951

The first thing a new-born child does is breathe, and the last thing a man does as his spirit leaves his body is stop breathing. Between these two extremes, the beginning and the end of life, we breathe every second of the day and night through weeks, months and years. We have discussed tuning and timing, and before tuning can be discussed advantageously it is necessary that we understand this whole subject of breathing.

There are many fads and fancies taught in the name of breathing, each one silly in itself but carrying weight with the voice student who has not learned that singing is a normal function of the human body.

For example, there is the log cabin method of breathing. Since Lincoln and Hayes were born in log cabins it therefore follows that one must study breathing only with a man who was born in a log cabin, and thus have the only true approach to the American way of breathing.

Then there is the Chinese Urn method of breathing. A great urn is placed in the middle of the studio and every voice student must imitate its shape, practicing each day to open his throat to the point of nausea. When he has mastered opening his throat in a flash to its widest extent, he has learned to breathe.

Next comes the method that makes good piano movers. The pupil lies on his back on the floor, and starts raising and lowering one brick placed on his abdomen. When he can easily raise one brick he gradually increases the number to a dozen. By so doing he is supposed to have mastered good breathing and, of course, should be able to use his abdomen to push pianos around.

Then there is the whistle method of breathing. A little whistle, such as one finds in teddy bears, is given the student at the first lesson. The whistle sounds the inhalation and exhalation. When he learns to take 24 steps to one intake of breath he has, so it is said, mastered perfect breathing.

We are also told of the method that advocates lifting the chest as high as possible, taking the posture of a pouter pigeon. And so on— and on!

Many years ago our class in Vocal Methods at Westminster Choir College made a survey of the different methods of breathing advocated in books on singing written largely by voice teachers. It was quite upsetting to the class to find that each book, almost without exception, approached breathing from a different viewpoint. We next made a survey of the subject as presented in books by great physicians. Without exception these books set forth the uniform idea "that man breathes to keep a normal supply of oxygen in the blood stream and to eliminate carbon dioxide." These medical books mentioned nothing about breathing for eating, sleeping, singing, athletic sports, or study. They gave but one reason for breathing, and that was the one stated above.

Why then is there so much confusion among students and teachers of singing? We believe this confusion has come about because those of us who teach, instead of studying the physiology of the body, have built up our own beautiful theories and fancies as facts. We forget that the teacher must necessarily talk two languages, the one understood by the performer and the other understood by the listener. For example, we say that the great singer sings on the breath, and so we tell our students that they must sing on the breath.

What we really mean is that the sound to the listener must seem to float through the air. We forget that sound has a normal speed at sea level of 1089 feet a second, or over 700 miles an hour. If we sing on our breath, as we so many times are told, our breath must travel at a speed of over 700 miles an hour, or at the speed of sound. A gentle June breeze that would have to travel even 60 miles an hour would be devastating. What would the same breeze do if it were traveling at the speed of sound, that is, over 700 miles an hour?

The truth is that sound waves move not on air, but move through air, in the same fashion that water waves move. If we throw a stone into the middle of a pond, the waves move out from the point of contact until eventually they ripple to the shore. The water itself does not move, but the energy created by the stone striking the water creates wave after wave. Just so, sound travels not on the air but through the air in successions of condensations until the initial energy of the vibrations is exhausted. We are told that in a voice free of interference the vibrations will travel as far as the singer can see.

If we breathe to keep up the normal supply of oxygen in the bloodstream and exhale to eliminate carbon dioxide, and if the breath does not leave the body when the vibrations leave the body, then we find that the old Italians were right when they placed a mirror or lighted candle in front of the mouth, and refused to accept the singing if the mirror clouded or the candle flame flickered. Both results showed that breath was escaping.

The problem for the singer, then, is to discover how to use the least amount of oxygen and how to create at the same time the greatest amount of energy that will travel in vibrations from his body at the speed of sound. Since medical scientists have studied the whole question of oxygen supply in the human body, it would seem wise for teachers of singing to build their teaching methods regarding the study of breathing upon the findings of these scientists. We learn that human beings use more oxygen when they are under emotional tension than they do at any other time. For example, air conditioning apparatus in theaters tends to break down when a large audience is witnessing a tense, emotional play. However, no such breakdown accompanies the showing of beautiful scenes in technicolor.

A large amount of oxygen is used by the mind. Physical activities use the least oxygen unless the emotional urge to win comes into play.

If we examine singing we find three different functions in man, working simultaneously and each one using up the oxygen supply. The first is the imaginative control of the great artist, who must constantly plan to so portray the music that the listeners are stirred emotionally. The second is the self-mastery of the performer who must hold firmly against the presence of hysteria or sentimentality in himself. And the third is the demand of the normal functioning of the body.

When we say that the great artist has mastered breathing, we mean that he has so mastered his self-control and has developed such poise

49

as to use up little of the oxygen supply that the blood stream must furnish to all parts of the body in order to carry on the normal function of just keeping alive. The natural functioning of the body is such that death comes almost simultaneously with the absence of oxygen. Even such a fundamental experience as tuning becomes impossible when the oxygen content in the blood stream is low.

Most of us have had the experience of climbing up a mountain and finding ourselves panting vehemently when we reached the top. Although we said we were short of breath, actually we were short of oxygen. Singers always find it next to impossible to sing in cities of high altitude until they have become acclimated to such heights. I remember one time some years ago when Westminster Choir arrived in Laramie, Wyoming, late in the afternoon and gave a concert that evening. Because of the shortage of oxygen we had difficulty keeping in tune, some had nosebleeds and none could hear.

The first thing a student must learn, whether he be a solo singer or a choir singer, is to decide what emotions he will allow to take control in his own mind and body. Fear is the first demon that must be faced and put down. Fear of sharps, fear of flats, fear of 16th or 32nd notes, fear of double dots, fear of so-called high tones or of so-called low tones, fear of long phrases, fear of pianissimo marks, fear of fortissimo marks. Each one of these little fears, so dear to many of us, must be mastered or each will take its toll of the normal oxygen supply of the body. Changing these fears has to do with knowledge and mastery of self, not with breathing. It seems to me that the first requisite in defeating fear is a good course in theory and in simple acoustics. To be sure there are many other pet fears, such as the fear of people—that they will laugh at us, criticize us, or talk about us. All of these make us "short of breath."

Courage is a fundamental requirement for every individual who expects to appear before people. To even begin the study of breathing the singer must have courage enough to forget self and focus his attention upon the pleasure of those to whom he is singing. With fear eliminated he will soon discover that no matter what his posture, what he eats, whether he is sleeping or awake, breathing goes on day and night without his volition. This realization will convince him that there is not much to worry about in breathing.

Before one can master the matter of breathing, he must accept the fact that air moves only under pressure, and that air enters the body only to equalize the pressure within and without the body. When the oxygen content is lowered and the carbon dioxide content is raised, a little organ at the base of the brain, called the medulla oblongata, bids the individual expel the air. The instant this is done the air pressure outside the body pushes new air in to keep the pressure inside and outside the same.

There is no vacuum and no vacuum pump in the body. Exhaling is the result of lowered oxygen content. Inhaling is the result of the air pressure outside the body being greater than that inside the body. Man has behaved this way since the day he was born. No thinking and no muscular control are required for correct breathing.

Correct Breathing for Singers:
Part Two
The secret of correct normal breathing lies in good posture

by John Finley Williamson

Etude Magazine, March 1951

To master correct breathing it is necessary to know how we breathe when we carry on with the normal functions of living. There is the breath of repose. We use it when we sleep, and when we are completely relaxed, but no one can sing or perform in public when he is completely relaxed. The sheer act of trying to say something through an art is as involved as is the art of music itself and requires great activity on the part of the performer. To discover how this activity is expressed put your thumb on the end of the sternum and your hand over the part of the abdomen that lies between the lines of the receding ribs on either side of your body. At the same time put your left hand at the side of the body on the lower rib line. Say "Oh!" first with the mood of quiet satisfaction, second with a mood of great weariness, next with a mood of longing, next with a mood of surprise, next with a mood of sudden irritation, next with a mood of tenderness. You will notice that each time you exclaim "Oh" for a different mood you make a different use of the muscles of the body.

Such observation proves that man has been so made up as to breathe in response to the various moods that go to make up the complex emotional life of man. He does this automatically because he is so made that the body constantly supplies the required amount of oxygen for all of the different moods that arise during a day of normal living. The poised individual is then the individual who controls the moods he uses during the day. The nervous, temperamental and sometimes hysterical individual is the individual whose moods control him. The nervous individual is always short of oxygen and is continually having a conflict within himself.

Joseph G. Beck

The singer then who wishes to be an artist must, above everything else, learn to discern and then project the moods the composer used when he created the music, and so it becomes the singer's task to make the public feel these moods. The beginning of breathing and the foundation of artistry rest then in breathing for each mood the singer expects to create. When this result is accomplished an amazing realization comes into the consciousness of the singer. He discovers that each mood has its own pace, and that if he breathes for a mood he not only has the right amount of oxygen in the blood stream but he has the feeling of the pace or the tempi in his muscles. He is then ready for the attack. So the formula for the singer or the conductor, for the pianist or the violinist, the woodwind or brass player, is the same. It is mood—breath—pace—attack.

Before we continue concerning breath control perhaps something should be said about muscles.

The diaphragm is a dome-shaped muscle that makes a solid airtight partition between the abdomen and the thorax. The diaphragm muscle is in reality two muscles. The one part is attached to the sternum in front and to the three upper lumbar vertebrae in the back. At the sides of the body it is attached to the six lower ribs and cartilages. The central part of the diaphragm is a tendon not attached to any bone. The diaphragm is one of the most powerful muscles in the body, and so functions that one cannot strike a blow, kick a football, throw a basketball or a baseball, or serve a tennis ball without the sternum giving a slight outward and upward bound and the ribs at the same time moving out a little from the sides of the body because of the action of the diaphragm. It also follows that we cannot sing a tone with vitality without a similar manifestation. This is not a cause, as is sometimes taught. This is a result of correct vital activity both in sports and in singing.

The secret of correct normal breathing lies in good posture, and the easiest way to achieve it is to lie flat on the floor with the entire spine touching the floor. If a sway-back condition keeps the spine from touching in its entirety it is good to raise the knees keeping the feet on the floor, causing the back to straighten until all parts of the spine meet the floor. Through this exercise of raising the knees the individual will gradually become able to keep the back straight. When this much is accomplished he should then stand against the wall with

54

the back still touching the wall in its entirety. Again he may have to bend the knees a little at the beginning. When the back is straight as the individual stands against the wall, the next step is to practice walking with this acquired posture. This posture is accepted by actors who must move about easily in a limited space and yet not attract attention to the movement. With such posture incorrect breathing is almost impossible. The individual will find that when he is relaxed there is a slight outward protrusion in the upper abdomen, but when he is active the expansion extends around the entire body. Especially is this activity noticeable in the back. The best way to observe perfect breathing is to put your hand around the waist of a baby and notice his breathing, then while he is lying on his stomach notice how his back expands in breathing, especially when he is very active and kicking. A child of three months has never studied voice, but its breathing is perfect. The important thing in studying breathing is not to worry about how we breathe but why we breathe. Breathing should give us self-control, it should give us poise, it should give us the ability to project the interpretative moods to the listeners.

After mood, breath and pace comes attack, and here again we have a lot of fads and fancies regarding so-called breath-control. In reading the different books on singing by vocal authorities, one would almost be led to believe that an individual could control certain muscles and thus feed air to the vocal cords. Too often we accept a detail of a whole and forget the whole. The whole is that any individual can only think of one thing at a time. When the artist sings, the only thought he can have is to so control the amplitude, softness and loudness of the tone so that beautiful phrasing is the result. If he thinks about breath and about breath control he must then believe that breath can be controlled and this we know is not true. Again may I repeat, the only conscious control a singer can have is that of the softness and loudness of the tone pattern that makes up the phrase. The voice is not the vibrations that move on a stream of air, the voice is not even sound made by the splitting of an air stream, as the tone of a flute. The vocal sound is the result of a vibration created by the approximation of the vocal cords. This approximation of the cords creates an obstacle that keeps the air from escaping, and in turn with the diaphragm builds air compression that causes the vocal cords to vibrate.

Breath control during correct singing means that the rate of expenditure of breath is controlled by the larynx while the diaphragm maintains the compression as the oxygen is exhausted. The whole activity around the waist then increases because of creating this air compression. The singer feels that his stomach and upper abdomen are being pulled in toward the spine. The entire upper chest wall is firm and on the high side. When the phrase is finished the individual needs to replenish quickly the entire supply of oxygen. This will immediately be taken care of through the air pressure outside the body. The singer then goes on to the next phrase.

The conductor of choirs must also accept his full responsibility for the good or bad breathing of his choir. In reality if the conductor has correct posture and breathes correctly, if he sings mentally all the time, the choir through empathy will do everything that he does. It is impossible for a choir to breath incorrectly if the conductor is right himself. This means also that correct posture must be a constant rule, both in performance and in rehearsals. One almost feels when he attends the rehearsals of a church choir that the singers are defying the Lord. They seem to say: "I give of my presence, that is enough. Don't expect me to use my intellect, my body or my imagination. It is too much to ask me to give of these if I give of my personal presence." The result is always boring to the performer and to the worshiper.

Singers when they sing must have both feet squarely on the floor, sit erectly on the chair with a feeling of almost lifting their bodies off the chair. This automatically brings about correct breathing, and with air compression used while singing, the result is always a beautiful tone, inspiring if the conductor or singer knows how to phrase artistically.

The Conductor's Magic

The group he directs is the choral conductor's instrument, and there is much to know about playing it. . .

by John Finley Williamson

Etude Magazine, April 1951

Some years ago, when my eldest grandchild was two years old, at the grandparents-showing-him-off-stage, we used to ask him to conduct. With a grin on his face, he would wave his arms frantically in the air. Since he had observed both his father and grandfather conduct, conducting to him was merely arm movement. I am not too sure that many of us in the conducting field do not have this same concept of conducting. However, waving the arms in the air is the least of a conductor's technique. He must be intelligent. He must be poised. And he must exercise over himself, as well as over the individuals who sing under his direction or who listen, absolute mastery and control.

Music-making today is an expensive business. Thousands of dollars are involved in a rehearsal of orchestra and choir. There is no time for anything that does not immediately and quickly produce the results the conductor demands. How much truth is embodied in a statement Sergei Koussevitsky recorded in the *New York Times* some ten years ago: "The conductor must be a professional athlete, a professional actor, a good psychologist and a great musician"!

The conductor must be able to stand on his feet from two to six hours a day. He must with his face, his hands and his body transmit to the performing group and through them to the audience all the feelings the composer has thought into the music. He must control the minds of the performing group so that the group becomes an instrument upon which the conductor plays and, through the control of sound, carries the emotional content to the listener. Since in larger groups each individual is so busy, so active and so mentally alert that he does not hear the other performers, the conductor must through his technique blend and fuse all sounds into white hot sound that glows with the magic of art and carries to the listener an aesthetic experience.

Unfortunately the many-sided responsibility of the conductor is not fully understood by some of us who attempt to conduct. Instead of achieving a sound that is white hot, too often we achieve a sound that is cold, clammy and out of tune and rhythm. Invariably we blame this unpleasant result upon the performing group or upon the acoustics of the hall or upon an unappreciative audience.

In reality no performing group can reach a level in performance higher than the concept of the conductor. Too often conductors classify themselves as band conductors, orchestral conductors or choral conductors when in reality, regardless of the medium, they must bear the responsibility of recreating the music of the composer. At 84 years of age Maestro Arturo Toscanini makes every individual in his immediate audience, as well as in his radio audience thousands of miles away, alive to the magic of his music. It would matter little whether he were conducting an orchestra, a band or a chorus.

Although the method of conducting remains constant whether one is conducting a choir or an orchestra, our interest in these articles pertains more specifically to the choral conductor. The technique of each individual singer varies just as the technique of the oboe player differs from that of the violinist or horn player, but the purpose still remains the creation of beauty through sound. The drill master is a very important man with specific responsibilities. However, we must not confuse his field with that of the conductor.

It is the drill master who should see that the choir is balanced as to parts, that it sings all time values correctly, that each individual in singing does not press, and so sharpen, the pitch, or relax and flatten the pitch. He must also see that acoustical laws are obeyed, so that the chords are always in architectural balance. He must see that diction is not an end in itself, but is a result of a phrase line that conveys the message of the poet and composer to the listener. When all these duties of the drill master have been accomplished the conductor is ready to begin his work.

It is a mistake to believe that in our conducting we must have points to our beats so that the choir can keep time. Singers do not keep time because of what they see. They keep time because of the forward-moving rhythmic pace the conductor creates through empathy. Then one sings under a great master he cannot make a mistake because he is too busy to stop and think. The conductor presses him forward with such electrifying power that he hasn't time to think how many beats he gives to a note or even what pitch he is singing. Everything in sound moves forward with such urgency that it is impossible to do anything other than the right thing.

If each one of us could cease projecting our individual ideas and accept the universal purpose and techniques of the great conductor, time beating would cease. A few weeks ago Mr. Koussevitzky conducted the Boston Symphony. Shortly after that he conducted the Israeli Symphony. The first orchestra was made up of musicians who had played under Mr. Koussevitzky for many years and knew his every movement. The second orchestra was made up of musicians of different tongues who had probably never seen Mr. Koussevitzky before, and yet they understood his language instantly because all great conductors speak the same language in movement, no matter where they conduct.

Each performer must know where the downbeat is in the measure so that he can count the measures while he is not performing. There may be 30 measures rest, yet he must come in without hesitation, with perhaps only an encouraging glance from the conductor. The first beat in a measure is always down, no matter what the pulse of the music, whether it be in *two*, *three*, or *four*. *Two*, or the second beat in a measure, is expressed differently in each pulse, and the instant each performer sees the second beat of the conductor he knows the pulse of the music. The upbeat is always the same because it leads to the down beat or to *one* in the measure, so really about all a conductor has to know about time beating is that *one* is down, that the second beat in *two*, *three*, and *four* pulse differs and that the last beat is always up.

The conclusion, then, is not that a great conductor has a correct pattern for time beating, but that he does not beat time. The only reason the performer must see the beat of the conductor is to know that the measure has begun and on what part of the measure the music starts. Richard Wagner said—and Arturo Toscanini said it again more recently—that the conductor's duty is to keep the pace or tempo.

59

The first important element in the conductor's responsibility, that of keeping tempo or pace, is often difficult since so many of us tend to think in terms of time, not rhythm. If we try to make our hands or baton go at the pace or speed at which we want the music to move and at the same time demand that the performer watch our movements we make it impossible for him to produce anything but a stiff, angular sound in music.

If we can accept that mood makes correct breathing and correct breathing gives us the pace then we have discovered the secret of movement in sound. I remember that once in a rehearsal with Mr. Toscanini, when we did not sing a certain passage in the tempo or pace he desired, he clasped his hands before his face in a gesture of prayerful supplication and gave the preparatory beat in such a way that we could not help but breathe for that mood. In the final performance he did the very same thing. I have many times noticed that Mr. Bruno Walter allows his singers to breathe only as he wishes. The result is that his music always glows with an inner feeling of spiritual intensity. A work like Bach's "St. Matthew Passion" speaks with fervor under Mr. Walter's direction because he makes his singers breathe for the mood demanded by the work.

If the conductor is interested in improving his conducting I should suggest that he become conscious of the different kinds of breathing for various moods by the following experiment. Place the thumb of the right hand on the sternum, or breastbone, with the fingertips of the same hand on the abdomen and the left hand on the left side ribs. Then speak the exclamation "Oh!" with quiet longing, with homesickness, with annoyance, with irritation, with amazement, with child-like wonder, and with tenderness. With this experiment will come the sudden discovery that each time one speaks he breathes differently. If he aspires to develop as a conductor, I suggest that he repeat this exercise each day, until he breathes naturally and instinctively for each mood.

Finally, when each member of the choir makes a similar discovery, it is wise to take a passage from an anthem that the choir knows from memory and to sing that passage portraying different moods. Suddenly like an inspiration, the choir will discover that they are reflecting the same facial expression and instinctively taking the same pace in breathing as the conductor. When this is carried through several phrases, the beginnings of good rhythm are established. Good rhythm begins as a physical response on the part of the performer to the mood and breathing of the conductor. Music does not change with every phrase, but has continuous pace. A good conductor is never erratic in his pace. He finds the pace of a certain passage and relentlessly makes the music hold to it without stopping at bar lines or for vowels or consonants.

The conductor dare not break the attention of the listener by making too sudden a change in pace. Therefore by facial expression he must prepare his choir for a new mood, a new beat, and a new pace. Through understanding and constant practice the choir can become a vital means of interpretation.

Planning a Choral Rehearsal
For best results, each step should be carefully mapped out in advance.

by John Finley Williamson

Etude Magazine, May 1951

No conductor nor choir can get very far without a definite rehearsal plan, and since the functions of the drill master and choir director, though very different, usually rest upon the same person we shall consider a plan for rehearsals which will recognize that for one part of a rehearsal period the individual in charge is the drill master and for the other part he is the conductor.

I have always found that it is best for singers to have particular chairs which they occupy at every rehearsal. They should be seated according to the parts they sing, and because a choir is seen before it is heard they should be seated according to their height and the color of their hair. If the choir sings eight-part music it is wisest to have the octaves in the middle, the second basses in the rear, the first sopranos in front of the second basses and both to the right of center, the first tenors in the rear and the second altos in front of the first tenors and both to the left of the center, the baritones to the right of the second basses, the second sopranos to the right of the first sopranos, the second tenors to the left of the first tenors, and the first altos to the left of the second altos. Within this seating each row should be arranged in a pleasing curve.

Each singer should find on his chair a folder marked with his name and containing the music for the next five weeks' rehearsals. We know psychologically that it is always wise to work from the known to the unknown. Therefore the first number to be sung would be that which is to be used at the next service. Naturally this is the fifth week this number has been rehearsed, so the leader will certainly be able to conduct it since the choir is by this time thoroughly conversant with music and text, and can follow his interpretation through shading and rhythm. Because the singers are so familiar with this number they soon lose the weariness that comes at the end of the day and begin the rehearsal with enthusiasm and verve.

The next anthem to be considered is anthem No. 5, which the choir has never seen. Before the choir members take this number from the folders the leader (who has now turned drill master), asks them to relax and close their eyes while he reads the text of the anthem with the moods he expects them to use when they sing the anthem in service five weeks hence. After the leader has finished reading, choir members, with eyes still closed, listen to the organist play it with the same interpretation that will be used in performance. If the leader and organist are two separate people, the leader must see that his organist is never asked to sight-read a number but that he has ample time to prepare it. The choir is now prepared to take the music from the folder and sing through it softly following the organ.

Upon the completion of the choir's singing of anthem No. 5, it is returned to the folder and anthem No. 4 is taken out. The previous week this number became a subconscious part of the singers as they heard the text, and listened to the music. The approach to all music should be with the ears and not with the eyes. The drill master now allows the choir to sing with a little fuller tone than he did the week before. He is on the alert for mistakes in time and intervals. If there are mistakes in time the section that makes them, or the entire choir if all are at fault, claps the time values vigorously to the organ accompaniment. As soon as the corrections are made they should again tap the time-values without the organ in a forward-moving rhythm. If intervals are wrong they should be corrected by the leader, who calls attention to the fact that they are the same simple intervals the choir has sung in other numbers.

Next anthem No. 4 is placed in the folder and anthem No. 3 is taken out. This is the third rehearsal for this number, and time values and intervals have all been corrected. Now the diction should be given particular attention. If the leader, on first reading the text, was careful as to diction, he will find that the greater part of what he desires in diction will have already been accomplished. All vowels should now be sung with the exact pronunciation that the dictionary gives. All consonants should be crisp. All articles, conjunctions, and unaccented syllables should be subordinated. Too many times we hear "Christ *The* Lord is Risen Today," and "Hol*ee*, Hol*ee*, Hol*ee*, Lord God

Almighty." If the music the choir is singing is good music the accents in the words and the accents in the music will be in accord and a new understanding of rhythmic flow will come to the choir.

Again anthem No. 3 is placed back in the folder and anthem No. 2 is taken out. The leader here is certainly a conductor. He should begin reading the text with the mood he will use when he conducts the number, and from then on the choir must watch his every movement and expression. Up to this time he has been more or less beating, or, if you wish, tapping time, but now he conducts. The choir must from his preparatory beat get the mood, breath, and pace. He does not lead them, he conducts with them, and they sing with him. He is neither ahead nor behind the group. They are all moving together in the recreation of the music as the composer intended it. The text suddenly takes on new meaning to choir members because now they sing not the dictionary's meaning of the words but the poet's meaning.

This pattern covering five numbers can just as well be expanded to ten or twelve, depending entirely upon how many numbers are in preparation. The wise leader should know how to secure a variation in the rehearsal period so as to create the greatest interest to the choir members. It has always seemed to me that a two-hour rehearsal proves most effective. It is absolutely necessary that the rehearsal start and stop at exactly the appointed time. It is a poor conductor who contributes to the carelessness of his choir members by allowing them to be late. I have sometimes overcome this tendency by charging the latecomers 5 cents a minute for each minute late, the money to be paid at the time the tardiness occurs. People hate paying for so simple a thing as being late.

At the end of 50 minutes of rehearsal, a 15-minute break is desirable. Perhaps during this 15-minute interval the choir would enjoy opening the windows and taking a few well-chosen physical exercises so as to supply the blood stream with more oxygen. During this break all announcements should be made both by leader and choir members. The second period should start exactly at the end of the 15-minute break. Two 50-minute rehearsals can accomplish more than 3 one-hour rehearsals if every member in the choir is kept interested and alert.

Between the various anthems new responses should be studied. The hymns for the Sunday service should be rehearsed. However, new responses and hymns should follow the same pattern and be in preparation for at least three weeks. Responsive readings should be studied and rehearsed. If the choir is not a church choir, I should advise that the leader take up at least one selection in choric speech with his groups. Ten or twelve minutes of the rehearsal given to choric speech will greatly sharpen clarity of diction.

I believe it is wise to rehearse all solos after the choir rehearsal is over. Just before the end of the rehearsal take up anthem No. 1 again. This is the 5th week for this number. It should open and close the rehearsal. The conductor should give everything he has to make this last singing of the number an inspiring, uplifting, and exhilarating experience for the choir. If this number is conducted properly, the choir members will feel that the rehearsal has been all too short because of the creative experience which has been theirs.

If the rehearsal has been that of a church choir it should close with a word of prayer. If it is a choir other than a church choir I still believe it should close with prayer, but if that is not desirable there should be no announcement or loud talking to destroy the uplifting experience that has come to the choir. Under such circumstances the choir members are certain to have something to remember and something to which to look forward at the next rehearsal.

Good Singing Requires Good Diction
Unless audiences can understand the words, choirmasters and singers are not doing their jobs properly.

by John Finley Williamson

Etude Magazine, September 1951

Choirs that sing in public should so sing that the people who listen hear music in all its parts, hear all the pitches and all of the time values; hear the beauty of the individual voices; hear the recreation of the mood that the composer felt when he created the music; hear and feel the meaning and the feeling of the text, and, at the same time, understand the text.

In these articles during the coming months, we wish to find the way of helping the individual singer, the choirmaster, and the choir singer who may read these articles to make people understand what the text is that he is singing. We must take for granted that the time values, the pitches, and the intervals are all correct and are all part of a forward moving rhythm. Enunciation and clarity of text must not be studied until these are established, as they are prerequisites to the study of good diction. They are prerequisites in every number that is sung.

A great, almost insurmountable, difficulty faces the average individual when he tries to sing. That difficulty arises from the fact that he has thought of our language as a language made up of letters and not a language made up of sounds. Any individual who is fortunate enough to have been taught spelling phonetically in the public schools has an advantage over those of us who have been taught to spell by letters. Some splendid authorities on music, when they attempt to give instructions to singers, are confused, and in their instructions they speak or write about the letter when the letter can have many different sounds. Last year one of our authorities put out a pamphlet which was sent to all the teachers of public school music in the United States. In this pamphlet he made the statement that the vowels were a, e, i, o, and u. Rather, he should have said that the vowel letters from which all vowels are formed are a, e, i, o, and u.

The letter "a" can be sounded as in faith, care, add, infant, father, or ask. The first one "faith" is a diphthong—the others are vowels. The letter "e" can be a vowel as in eve, as in event, as in end, as in silent, or it can be the diphthong as in they. "I" is another peculiar sound which also has different uses. It can be the diphthong as in ice, or it can be the vowel sound as in ill. "O" can have the vowel sound as in lord, as in odd, as in dog, as in occur, or the sound of it as in women, or it can be used as the diphthong as in go. "U" has the sound as in hub, or the sound as in circus, or can be used as a diphthong as in duty or unite. Beyond the shadow of a doubt, we are safe in saying that the letters a, e, i, o, and u are not vowels. They must have sound before they become vowels and diphthongs.

If the one who sings or the one who conducts, when he looks at a word, can hear the sounds and not think of the letters, a large part of his battle for good diction will be over. For example, the simple word "of" is not sounded with "o" and "f," but with the vowel in the sound as in the word "sod" and the consonant sound of "v." The word "lord" is not sounded l-o-r-d, but is sounded with the sustained vocal sound given to the letter "l," the vowel as in "saw," the r silent, and a quick "du" ending the word. "Who" is never sounded w-h-o, but is sounded with a quick "h" and the "oo" as in soon.

The definition of phonetics, according to the dictionary, is as follows: "The science of speech sounds considered as elements of language; especially the study of their formation by the speech organs and apprehension by the ear, their attributes, and their relation to other aspects of language; also, the application of this science to the understanding and speaking of languages."

The one who sings or the one who conducts singing must so master the phonetics of the English language or whatever language he is using, that he spins a continuous line of sound that is made up of each sound in the word and, in turn, in the phrase. A good illustration is a string of pearl beads. The strong thread going through the pearls is the vitally emotionalized breath of the performer. The beads themselves are the vowels and the diphthongs. The beads touch each other but between each bead is a space—that space represents the consonants. The only weakness in this illustration lies in the fact that there is space between the beads. One of the weaknesses in our English language is that the consonant p, the consonant t, and the consonant k make a space between the sounds because these consonants are noises.

John McCormack once said that the greatest art is the art that conceals itself. He meant the art that conceals the fact that perfect legato is not possible in singing because of the consonants p, t, and k. The singing voice must have such a bound legato that one is conscious only of a continuous phrase in which every sound is heard. With this continuous phrase the softness and loudness (or the amplitude) must be so controlled that the form of each phrase is beautiful, bearing out the climaxes of the construction of music. When this is done, we have laid out the foundation for good diction and the beginnings of artistry.

Another wonderful phenomenon is present with this legato singing of vowels and consonants. The voice ceases to make you conscious of words as words or words as tones, rather the voice makes you conscious of thoughts in phrases and beauty in the tone that makes up the entire phrase.

The voice that is most easily understood is the voice of the child 5, 6, 7 years of age. This clarity of enunciation may even continue until the voice changes. As soon as the youthful individual tends to imitate or starts to study voice too young or with a poor voice teacher, clarity of enunciation disappears.

Any kind of time beating that lays emphasis upon a single note or a single word will destroy this clarity of enunciation. Each one of us who conducts must conduct through a phrase, not stopping on the individual beats. The child in the average class in public school music and in the average junior choir has no possible chance of keeping his childlike clarity of enunciation in phrasing, because of the time beating of the individual who leads his group.

The thought of the individual singer singing alone or in a group must be, not to say words, but to sing phrases in which all of the sounds are so woven together that the meaning and the feeling of the phrase goes to the listener. In this way we know that we clearly comprehend the word, and are very sure that the clarity of the enunciation is right. In doing this the quality of tone of the individual singer changes completely.

Individuals who, in singing, sing a word to a beat always give out sounds that are sharp, thin, and almost strident. Individuals who sing phrases always give out sounds that are rich and colorful produced entirely in relation to the feeling of the phrase that they are singing. If the singer or the conductor wishes to have a beautiful quality of tone in his choir no matter what the age of the group is, he can very easily achieve this desire. All that he needs to do is to make of each phrase a legato line in which every sound is present in its relative value. The ability to do this depends entirely upon the thinking of the performer, be he singer or conductor.

To master this, the singer or conductor must know all the vowels of the English language, must know all of the consonants of the English language. He must so practice these that their correct use becomes instinctive. To be instinctive, we mean that their correct use must be reflected in daily speech. One cannot speak carelessly all day and then sing beautifully for a half hour or hour at night. Each time the organs of speech are used, the laws of phonetics must be obeyed, and since these laws are natural laws that came into being through the centuries past in the development of language, one must learn to obey these laws instinctively. However, it is not an easy task but will take careful, conscientious, and correct mental obedience to these laws in daily speech and daily singing.

In my next article, we shall take up the study of the fourteen vowel sounds in the English language. Following that we shall study the six diphthongs, and following that we shall study the consonants in all their varied sounds and usages. This article and the articles that follow will, in reality, be studies in phonetic spelling because good singing means that the individual spells phonetically and applies his softness and loudness through the phonetical line of sound. He does this obeying the laws of good style and always reflecting good taste. If these sounds are heard by the listener when he speaks and when he sings, we call him an artist.

The Importance of Vowel Coloring

Correct pronunciation of vowels in singing helps to create the mood which the composer intended.

by John Finley Williamson

Etude Magazine, October 1951

The artist in public speaking and the artist in singing are alike in many ways. The public speaker has this advantage, that he can create his own pitch and rhythm whereas the singer must accept the pitch and rhythm of the composer. Both are alike in that everything that the listener hears comes on the sounds of vowels, diphthongs, and consonants. When you listen to the great artist in speech or song you are never conscious of the words, rather you are conscious of the thought of the phrase. This means that the inspiring singer must thoroughly understand the elements in good diction. To understand these elements it is necessary that he thoroughly master phonetic spelling by sound and not by letter. Those of us who have been taught from our early youth to spell by letter are greatly handicapped when we take up this study. Our brain has been taught to hear with our eyes and not with our ears.

Last week I was with a good friend who is completing his thesis for a Doctor of Philosophy degree. He conducts a splendid choir. He is the head of a music department in a strong college, and yet this gentleman was born blind. He has never seen himself in a mirror. He has never seen light and yet he is one of the most sensitive individuals it has been my privilege to know. A part of his thesis is given over to explaining how blind people see. As he explains it, they see with their ears, with their sense of touch, their sense of taste, and their sense of smell. The psychologists tell us that blind people are more intelligent than deaf people because greatest intelligence comes when all of the senses are used, not just the sense of sight. This gentleman reflects that sensitivity or intelligence. He sings with beautiful diction and plays with beautiful tonal quality. Without seeing his choir, he can tell them instantly what they are doing that causes them to sing incorrectly, and without a spoken word he can make his choir sing in rhythm and with a good quality of tone because he has mastered himself so thoroughly that his mind through the ears knows everything that is happening and instinctively he coordinates to produce the result that he desires.

In giving this long example I hope that you who read this article will learn to see without eyes, will learn that the letter "o" is not o. It has many sounds. The letter "e" is not e. It has many sounds, and so for all the other vowels. When you learn how to hear all vowel sounds you must be sure that what you accept is right according to the dictionary usage. Our language has developed through the centuries through usage, and events in past history have helped make what is to us natural in our expression today.

About thirty years ago Mrs. Williamson and I were traveling in Germany from the city of Hamburg to the German capital, Berlin. In the compartment with us sat two heavy gentlemen dressed in black. Next to them and directly across from us sat a well-dressed man that we knew to be German. Mrs. Williamson and I carried on a conversation with this German gentleman and the two gentlemen next to the window kept getting more and more excited. At last they broke into the conversation speaking very excitedly to the German gentleman. They told him that they knew we were American and that they understood a great many of our words. He explained to us that they were farmers from Denmark and suddenly they had realized that they understood many of our words. There was a logical explanation of this. In the years 871-901 the Danes crossed the channel and conquered England. They brought many new words that became a part of our English language. From reading our lips and hearing the sounds, our fellow travelers recognized those words. After 1,050 years, people who seemingly have no kinship in country or language found that they had a kinship in both language and country.

Our discussions here are solely with the pronunciation that comes to us from the dictionary. The dictionaries vary little whether they be English or American. We many use the word "baby buggy." The English say "perambulator." Our dictionary may say "streetcar." The English dictionary may say "tram," but correct speech reflects culture and our dictionaries, both in English and American, being the repository through the centuries of a growing culture, will have almost the same pronunciation.

As I present these vowel sounds to you, you will notice I present them as words, all but one starting with the sibilant "s" and that one starting with the sibilant "f." The reason for the use of the sibilant is two-fold. First, it makes the words easier to remember, and second the sibilants having a much higher pitch value than vowels or consonants make it more easily possible for individuals who have speech impediments to produce the correct vowel sounds in the word. At the same time it helps those who speak and those who sing in a habit pattern, because they have used no intelligence, to find a way out of this rut into a pattern of creatively controlling the sounds that they use.

In the English language our dictionary gives us the classification of twelve vowel sounds and two diphthong sounds that are often classed as vowel sounds, making fourteen in all. The fourteen sounds can be heard through speaking the following words:

soon—sew—saw—psalm—say—see—swirl
soot—sod—sung—sat—set—sit—fast

Twelve of these are pure vowel sounds. The other two, sew and say, are called vowels but in reality are diphthongs.

The Italian language is a beautiful language. Most authorities say that the elder Lamperti, an Italian, was the world's greatest voice teacher. Many of our great voice teachers have been Italians. In the Italian language the letter "o" as in "so" is a vowel with the sound as in the word "saw." Likewise, the letter "a" as in "say" or the letter "e" as in "they" is a vowel sounded as in the word "set." Personally, I have felt that because we so idealize the Italian voice teachers we have very gradually allowed ourselves to believe that these sounds are vowels. In the Italian language they are vowels. In the English language they are diphthongs. A diphthong is a vowel sound that merges into a second vowel sound. The first vowel sound is sustained, the second vowel sound is a gradually disappearing vowel sound. The two elided together make up what we call a diphthong.

Too often in directing a choir or in teaching an individual to sing, we go on the assumption that there is one "ah" vowel as in psalm, one "e" vowel as in see, one "oo" vowel as in soon, one "o" vowel as in sew, one "a" vowel as in say, and one "i" vowel as in sigh. This faulty assumption immediately makes the singer's diction clouded because it limits the vowels used to these few vowel sounds. This immediately confuses the listener because in listening to spoken English, we are used to the two "oo" vowels, "soon" and "soot." We are accustomed to hearing the "ah" vowels as in "sod," "psalm," "saw," "fast," with the closely related vowel sounds as in "sung," "sat," and "swirl." We are accustomed to the two "e" vowels as in "see" and "sit" and the one closest to them as in "set."

In mastering good diction, it is absolutely essential that we first learn to use these twelve vowels correctly according to dictionary usage. The choir director and the singer should make it a habit to use the dictionary continually every time a new number comes into rehearsal. He should be absolutely sure before he enters rehearsal that he knew the correct vowel sound to use in each word that he or his choir will sing. It will help the choir greatly if in the tuning of the choir these words are used, not tuning the choir just on one vowel sound or humming but making them tune on all vowel sounds even though to the singer the vowels produce in him the same sensation. When the leader seriously takes up the study of vowel purity this tuning should be carried on two or three times during the rehearsal. In fact, it should be continued until the singers seem to instinctively sound all vowel sounds correctly and until the words come to the listener through the thought of the phrase rather than through the impulse or accentuation of individual syllables and individual words.

When this has been realized we are ready for the study of mood in vowel purity. No vowel sound can be correctly produced unless it carries the color of the mood that the composer felt then he created the music. When we use a mood of joy our entire sentence has a different vowel color and a different inflection from that used in the mood or sorrow. Exultation carries on mood and brings to the sound a mood color that is entirely different from that of contrition. Tenderness brings it own mood color to the sentence. To the eye there are thousands of different shades and colorings. To the ear there are also thousands of different shades and colorings.

Each vowel sound on each half step throughout the range of the voice of the singer will have a slightly different color if all vowel sounds are pronounced according to the dictionary. If all of these colors are then multiplied by the number of different moods that may be used, we can then see the infinite possibilities for richness and vocal coloring. We also immediately realize why our English language is one of the most beautiful languages, if not the most beautiful language in the world. To achieve these results, correctness of vowel sounds in daily speech and singing must become instinctively right according to the dictionary. Then instinctively and very naturally the moods of the text and of the music will give their added richness and greatly increased beauty to the singing of the individual or of the group.

***Editor's Note: See "A Singer's Guide to Diction in the English Language: from lectures and writings by John Finley Williamson" for a more in depth study on diction.

The Choral Conductor
The Singer

by John Finley Williamson

Lectures at Westminster Choir College, Summer 1959

Introduction

All of art must come from the heart. This must be true because the quality that makes art endure is the spiritual value that must be in art. The art that comes most quickly from the heart and speaks most readily to the heart is the art of music—in particular the art of solo and choral singing. In the last movement of the Ninth Symphony of Beethoven, in which he has set Schiller's great poem, these words ring out: "All men are brothers." Paul has said: "And He made of one blood all nations of men for to dwell on all the face of the earth." Those of us who deal with the art of singing must recognize that voices are not national but cosmopolitan; voices are not Oriental or Occidental, but human. They come through the human throat, from the human heart and mind.

Through the years we have been privileged to give concerts in almost every country in Europe and in almost every country in the Orient, Asia, and the Near East. Without exception we find the people that make up audiences react in the same way. All peoples who listen to music are moved and react with enthusiasm to the music if their entire faculties—body, heart, and mind—are brought into activity by the music to which they are listening. First, if their bodies are in tune rhythmically with the music being created by the singers, their response is immediate. Second, if the mood of the music creates a drama in the text, their emotions and their hearts are immediately stirred. Third, if the singer or the conductor can, through his own good taste, create beautiful phrases and outline the form of the composer, their minds are stimulated and inspired. This must all be accomplished and realized through the vowels and consonants that make up the text. The realization of all of this is the same in every language.

Joseph G. Beck

We have been privileged through the last eighteen years to have sung 122 performances with the New York Philharmonic Symphony Orchestra. During that same time we had about 80 performances with other symphony orchestras, such as The Symphony of the Air and the Philadelphia Orchestra. We have been privileged to have had about 45 performances under the baton of Bruno Walter; 25 under Arturo Toscanini; about 30 under Leopold Stokowski; many with Dimitri Mitropoulos, many with Eugene Ormandy, many with Rodzinski, many with Rachmaninoff, with the late Guido Cantelli and with Charles Muench, the great conductor of the Boston Symphony. We have sung all of the great masterpieces in all different languages, but whenever we were able to realize fully the music as I outlined in the three points above, the conductors were delighted and the audiences were pleased. To achieve that fully we have found that, without exception, the conductors first established the mood that they would use; then set the breathing for the orchestra and the choir that automatically gave to the orchestra, the choir and the audience the pace of the music; then the attack was given and the conductor immediately, in his control of amplitude, controlled the vowels and consonants. The releases always were a part of the rhythmic pattern.

Great masters like Toscanini and Bruno Walter are almost ruthless in their making these demands upon the orchestra and the choir, because they know then exactly how the audience will receive the music. In this all too brief time that I shall have the pleasure of working with you, I wish then to follow this pattern: mood—breath—pace—attack—vowels and consonants under control of amplitude—release. The few brief lectures that I give will follow these topics. Every class in choral technique and in choral conducting will follow these subjects; and when I conduct you I shall use this as a pattern. This is in entire accordance with the great maestros of the past. Berlioz said, "The conductor may only set the tempi and control the softness and loudness." Richard Wagner says in his book on conducting, "The conductor has the right only to control the tempi and the melody to the fore." This means that the only privilege that a conductor has is that of setting the pace and controlling the amplitude, or the softness and loudness, or the dynamics; or to keep the melody to the fore. It must be the singer's or the choir's responsibility to keep the pace, to follow the conductor's control in amplitude; but the singer—individually or collectively—must in keeping the pace keep the music rhythmic; must realize all vowels and consonants in a phrase pattern; and must realize the music exactly as the composer put it on the page. Therefore, greatness in music rests, first, with the composer; second, with the singer or performer; and last, with the conductor.

I. Mood

An individual who lives by his emotions has a difficult time in the process of living. The wise man is the one who controls his life by controlling his emotions. The individual who does not control his emotions lives erratically; therefore the man who controls his emotions may at the same time experience the mountain-peaks and the valleys of exciting living. Art consists of portraying emotion through mood to the listener or the viewer. Therefore, the singer or the conductor is responsible for discovering the moods that the composer wished to convey when he created the music. The singer or the conductor is then a recreator and responsible not for expressing his own feelings but for the recreation of the moods desired by the composer. Music without text can arouse different moods in different members of an audience. Music that is well wedded to text has the double power of text and the suggestion of mood—moods such as tenderness, aspiration, exultation, inspiration, tender grief, poignant grief, deep sorrow, courage, joy that brings tears, joy that brings laughter, joy that comes from looking at your first child, joy that comes from looking at your first grandchild, joy that comes from the discovery that all men are brothers, relentless purpose, all of the many very beautiful forms of love and affection, thanksgiving in all of its beautiful forms, and so on for in all of its sorrow, in all of its exultations. In our daily life we express these moods in conversation, we express these moods in all of our family life, and the expression always comes through the natural and subconscious control of breathing. The performer must be at all times in his performance an actor who uses the lower jaw of an idiot and the upper jaw of an artist. If he becomes emotional personally, his lower jaw becomes tense; if he projects mood intelligently, the lower jaw becomes as free and loose as that of an idiot. If we study the faces of the great men and women who love their fellow men—such as religious leaders, great physicians, great leaders in government, great actors—we find this type of freedom in the lower jaw, with an activity in the forehead and around the eyes and the upper lips. In addition to this change in the facial expression, there is a complete change in breathing for each mood that is used. The individual can easiest discover this for himself if he will put his left hand on the bottom of his lower left ribs, put his right hand on the triangle that is formed between the bottom of the sternum and the ribs on the left and right side. If he then uses an exclamatory sound, such as "Oh!" with the mood of quiet longing, extreme longing, tender grief, tumultuous grief, sudden quiet irritation, sudden very annoying irritation—he will make a very exciting discovery. For each mood his upper face will change; but even more important, he will discover the fact that his breathing for each mood will be very different in two ways—the length of time that he takes for the breath, and the different movements that will be made by the ribs and the upper abdominal wall.

No individual should attempt to sing or conduct until he has mastered this concept and experience. Many of our greatest conductors have been violinists or cellists. Many of our greatest singers are individuals who first prepared for a career as a performer on the violin or cello. On these two instruments the performer must pre-place in his entire body the pace of the music. He does this entirely through breathing, and before he breathes he must know what he wishes to say in mood. If he does not do this he is only a mechanic. The late Serge Koussevitsky, who made the Boston Orchestra so wonderful, once said that a conductor must first be a professional athlete; second, be a professional actor; third, a professional psychologist in his dealings with people; and last, a professional musician. Everything that the singer, the conductor, the actor, the professional speaker in any walk of life does, depends upon his portrayal of mood; but in music he must portray the mood that someone else has created. Therefore, he is not a creator, but a recreator. This ability will help his listeners to find the mountain-peaks of experience in listening to his music.

II. Breathing

One of the most sublime experiences of my life was when I was privileged to watch the birth of my son. The instant after he was born the doctor slapped him, and suddenly a cry came. I wanted to observe how he started life. His independence started when he made that cry. The breath preceded the cry. From that time on until he was about eighteen months of age, the breathing was automatic and almost perfect. One of the fundamental faults in singing is that we try to make our breath conscious instead of subconscious and instinctive. We forget that when we are born our breathing is perfect; that when we sleep our breathing is perfect; all during the day whenever we talk our breathing goes on automatically without our thought. It's only when we try to sing that we start making very unusual mistakes in thinking about breathing, with a very unpleasant result in the sound that comes from our throats. Many of us believe that we can control our breathing. Many of us believe that we can control the amount of air that we take in and the amount that we force out. We often hear the phrase that we must sing on our breath; that the sound comes to the listener supported by a column of breath; that we must very steadily emit the air so that our tone will be steady. The truth is that our breathing must obey fixed physical and natural laws, and when we break those laws not only our singing but our health and our mental outlook suffer.

The first law is that <u>air moves only under pressure</u>. It is the varying pressures that make windstorms. <u>These pressures are the same inside of the body as they are outside of the body</u>. If the pressures in the body should be lowered beyond what they are outside of the body, the lungs would collapse. If the pressures inside of the body should be increased over the pressures that are outside of the body, the lungs would burst. The lungs are made of very delicate cells, almost like tiny balloons. Their combined surface is over three times the skin surface of our entire bodies. Our lungs have no strength or power within themselves.

The second law is that <u>our breathing is automatic</u>, and the <u>control is in the pressures outside of the body</u>; because the pressures must be the same inside of the body as they are immediately around the body.

The third law is that the act of <u>breathing is the act of taking in oxygen and eliminating carbon dioxide</u>. Oxygen is the great life-giving element that we all need and must have. If suddenly all of the oxygen were drawn out of the air, we would in a few seconds be dead. If we were suddenly transported 12,000 feet high to a mountaintop,

81

we would gasp and gasp and gasp, not for breath, but for oxygen. The airplane is a wonderful creation of man's ingenuity and creative thinking, but if we should go too high in a non-pressurized cabin we would quickly become unconscious because of shortage of oxygen, and in about seventeen seconds would be dead. A pressurized cabin means that the oxygen content in the air is kept up artificially so that we can breathe and live normally.

The secret then for the artist—be he singer or conductor—is so to control his thinking and his expression of moods that he uses as little oxygen as possible. To do this the individual must definitely know how to so plan his life that he does not continually lose oxygen. If we make this study, we find that in air-conditioned theaters the air-conditioning breaks down when the emotional content is great. We know then that the expression of emotion uses up the most oxygen. Sustained, exalted thinking is next in its use of oxygen; and physical activity uses the least oxygen. We at our college in Princeton have just built a new dormitory that will care for 120 students. The rooms have been designed so that each room is large enough to allow two men to study steadily from two to four hours, and always have enough oxygen to sustain the activity of their brains. The heating and ventilation of each room is under separate control so that each student can know for himself what is right in oxygen control for himself and his roommate. <u>The truth then is that man does not control his breathing, but he controls the moods and the desires that dominate his life</u>. The singer and the conductor must then <u>control and create the moods that the composer felt when he created the music</u>. This act controls the breathing.

The physical secret in correct breathing is revealed in the fact that correct posture makes the physical activity correct. The diaphragm is the most powerful muscle in the body. It cannot be controlled consciously. It works perfectly at birth, but if the singer or conductor tries to interfere with that natural breathing his work suffers. We hear different individuals talk about high chest breathing, abdominal breathing, intercostal breathing, diaphragmatic breathing. As we have stated above, the individual who has correct posture and who breathes to create mood, will be able to forget the problems that we think we have with breathing; but more than that, he can have the joy of correct physical, mental and spiritual coordination. In addition to having this joy, he can have the joy of seeing fears removed. The right spelling of the word fear should be s-i-n, or sin, the fears that come when you look at a long phrase, the fears that come from singing a note that seems high on the staff, the fears that come from singing a note that seems too low on the staff, and all the little fears that bother singers and sometimes conductors. All of these fears will disappear when the singer and the conductor in a positive way select the mood, and breathe for that mood. Good posture is so necessary, and good posture is the posture that you see in all actors and actresses. Especially is that true in all who are in the movies. All good athletes will have good posture. It simply means standing erect, and standing tall without tension. The returns are great—health, freedom from fears, and joy in living.

III. Pace

The words pace and tempi are two very important words in music. Mood becomes a reality for the listener through the pace and the forward rhythmic progression of pitch duration. By pitch duration I mean the time value that is given to each note. The Metronome was discovered in Beethoven's lifetime; and since that time most composers have put Metronomic markings on their music—such as 72, 80, 90—to indicate whatever tempo they wish used in relation to a Metronome. Richard Wagner refused to do this. He said that if a performer could not find the pace of his music from the music, he was not a good enough musician to perform his music. The tragedy of Metronome markings is that if a conductor follows the markings he thinks 1-2-3-4 in 4/4 time, or 1-2-3 in 3/4 time, etc; and that is all that he does think, and we call him a time-beater. You can only find the pace of a number from studying the music and the text; and when you find it that way you have discovered the mood that the composer tried to portray. If you watch a good violinist and a good cellist, you can tell from his breathing how fast he will play. If you watch the back of a good conductor, he announces to the audience the pace of the music through the breathing in his back, at the same time that he announces it through his face and chest to the choir or the orchestra. This is one of the two privileges that a conductor has, the other privilege being the control of the amplitude. However, the conductor does not keep the pace. After he announces the pace through his breathing, the keeping of the pace is entirely the responsibility of the choir or the orchestra. If a conductor time-beats, there can be no pace, only a monotonous, dead, dull, steady beat.

The one great law that every clergyman, every public speaker, every actor, every musician, and every athlete must obey, is the law of empathy. The law of empathy, as used in dramatics, is that the listeners or audience unconsciously react with the performers. Sympathy is feeling for, and no performer wants sympathy; empathy is feeling with the performer. The conductor who allows the choir to keep the pace will find that they are immediately obeying the law of empathy and are feeling with him. His whole body then must be in the same rhythmic procession and the same pace that the choir or orchestra and audience are creating. This means that temperamentalism and sentimentalism have no place. The interpretation must obey the laws of beauty and good taste and good style. This also means that not for one second may the conductor's mind wander from what he is doing, nor may the singer's mind wander from what he is doing.

Rhythm we know is muscular. Pitch is memory. Time values must be realized as pitch duration and must be always a part of rhythm. Diction is subconscious, and that also must be realized as a part of the rhythmic progression. That means that the conductor's mind and the performer's mind must be entirely upon pace and amplitude. Amplitude, or softness and loudness, or dynamics, makes shading and makes rhythm. Rhythm is not regular recurring accent. Rhythm is a pattern of crescendo and diminuendo that starts with every sixteenth note and always moves forward, portraying the mood of the music.

IV. Attack

Simple words can have many meanings. One of these simple words is the word attack. It can mean physically attacking an individual. It can mean starting together. In music it usually is taken to mean starting together; as we say, the attack of the choir, or the orchestra, was good. In singing and in choral music, however, it has only one meaning; and that is the sound that issues from the throat of the individual when his vocal chords meet. Garcia, perhaps the world's greatest teacher of singing, has said that attack can be wrong in stroke of the glottis, in pitch and in formation, and that it can only be right when it is a shock of the glottis. If the attack is faulty in pitch, it is also faulty in formation; if it is faulty in formation, it is also faulty in pitch. This comes when the mouth changes shape after the pitch starts. The greatest difficulty with changing the mouth is in the incorrect articulation of consonants. In all languages the jaw should not move except on consonants that are made with the lips, such as m, p, b, and f and v in some languages. The lips may move, but not the jaw. When a column of air is set in vibration, the shape of the column must not change. If the shape is made larger the pitch will flat; if it is made smaller the pitch will sharpen. If pace is kept through control of rhythm, usually the faults of faulty attack in pitch and formation will leave.

The stroke of the glottis is the most dangerous because that makes a clicking sound before the vowel and, if persisted in, will cause hoarseness that can become chronic. The shock of the glottis is correct and means that the chords immediately, in accordance with mood, breath and pace, touch and start vibrating. This, however, means the acceptance on the part of the singer or the conductor of certain fundamental laws. First, the phenomenon we call voice or sound is a combination of even and uneven frequencies, or vibrations. Vibrations travel in all directions at the same time and at the same rate of speed. I think that is 760 miles per hour at sea level, the speed of sound. The sounds that are made by the human being in this respect obey the same laws that the violinist, the oboist, the trumpeter, etc., obey. Law number two, the voice does not travel on the breath but travels through the ether around us in all directions, at the speed of sound. The breath does not leave the body. The old Italians placed a candle or a mirror before the mouth. If the flame flickered or the mirror clouded, the breath was escaping and the tone was wrong. Correct attack keeps the breath from escaping from the body, but does not keep the performer from becoming short of oxygen. That rests on the performer's own controls of his fears and his breathing. If vibrations that are traveling at the speed of sound are electrified, they will travel 186,000 miles a second, as they do in radio. Therefore, we are very sure that voice cannot be placed; for I know if I broadcast while I am with you in Japan, the people in the United States can hear me before the people sitting in the broadcasting studio would hear me, and every vibration travels at the speed of sound; noise doesn't. Therefore, I would be safe in saying that he who knows how to breathe and has correct attack can sing well if he finds out for himself what instinctive pronunciation of vowels is.

V. Amplitude

All of singing, either solo or choral, comes to the listener through vowels and consonants. When we say that the conductor's task is announcing or setting the pace and controlling the amplitude, we mean that he must do all of this in choral music through vowels and consonants that the singers produce. Therefore, a solo tone or a choral tone, as it comes to the listener, is the combined color of all the vowels and all the consonants. Since tone in singing is vibration and obeys the laws of vibration, we must accept the fact that vowels are vibrations. Consonants we shall discuss later. If vowels are vibrations, and these vibrations are made entirely in and by the vocal chords, then it is very right that we find some of the problems involved. The great problem arises when we are forced to accept the fact that the duration of pitches—such as A-440 or A-220 or A-880 or C-254—are the fundamental matters to be concerned in developing the melody or the harmony. The pitch of each melody being right, we must add to this the overtones that go with that fundamental melody tone, that make the timbre of the voice. This arouses great difficulty because timbre in instruments is accepted as overtone, but when it comes to voice, individuals pay no attention to what we call timbre, but think it is some gift that comes to them at birth. For example, if you purchase an oboe or a bassoon, the company from which you purchase the instrument will guarantee the overtones or harmonics in the instrument, because the thing that makes the instrument is the elimination or the retention of certain overtones. The same is true of brass instruments. The same is true of strings, as we pay the greatest price for the stringed instrument that has the most beautiful combination of harmonics or overtones, or the most beautiful tone. Since voices must obey the same laws that instruments obey, voices also must have overtone. The easiest voice to deal with in this respect is the bass voice, because in a good bass singer you can hear up to the thirteenth harmonic. Tenors have fewer overtones that can be heard, altos fewer yet; and sopranos, because their frequencies lie so high, have the same overtones as the bass, but fewest can be heard because they go beyond the range of the human ear; hence the soprano voice is the dullest or darkest voice. This reality of overtones must be taken into account when you build a choir. This means that in choir work the bass section is the most important. If they sing with overtone, it makes it very easy for the other voices in the choir to keep their pitch. In fact, Scherchen goes further in that he says that in modern music no note may be used in harmony or melody that is not in the overtone system of the bass note.

But having a choir in tune is not enough. To the fundamental frequency of the music itself and to the system of overtones that make timbre must be added the system of overtones that make vowels. Each separate vowel that is used, no matter what the language, has its own combination of frequencies. This result is achieved by the singer, not through trying to say words, but through recognizing that the whole question of vowel color as it is expressed in the dictionary is the result of centuries of usage by individuals. Every child when it first starts speaking, in any language, immediately finds how to make the different vowel sounds; but he does this because all of this is controlled in the speech center of the brain, and this control is subconscious and automatic. If we can accept the fundamental pitch of the melody or the harmony, the pitches or frequencies that make timbre, and the pitches or frequencies that make vowels, we then are ready to start the study of the use of vowels in singing.

Lamperti, the elder, said that "he who knows how to breathe and how to pronounce knows how to sing." My three great teachers—Witherspoon, Bispham, and Green—were all students of Lamperti. By breathing he meant breath to control pace. By pronunciation he meant learning to pronounce vowels subconsciously in the instinctive, natural, childlike way of children before their voices change. In reality, vowel production, when it is correct in a singer, is close to the grunting sound of uh, as in SUNG. When an individual listens to a singer he does not understand the words because he consciously hears every vowel and consonant; but he understands the words through association of ideas. Having every vowel and every consonant in the continuous line of sound is necessary, for otherwise you do not have

87

legato; and therefore it is necessary for the sake of legato and phrasing, not for the sake of clarity in diction.

With this foundation laid, the conductor is then ready to consider that control of softness and loudness makes rhythm, and rhythm carries mood. The only thing that the singer can think of is keeping the pace and the control of amplitude. If his vowels and consonants are all subconsciously flowing in a melodic line that is continually moving forward in rhythm through the shadings or variations of amplitude, we can quickly see that, though this is not a simple matter, if the above principles are accepted it can be a comparatively easy matter for the conductor or the singer to achieve.

If the conductor does not at any time time-beat, but follows a pattern of hand movement that never ceases, he then can give his attention to the crescendo and diminuendo, because the movements of his hands will keep the same pace as the pace of the music.

The release must always be in rhythm and is the responsibility of the singer or the choir.

Before we close we must, however, face the question of drama in singing. Drama in singing comes into being through the control of consonants. The singing is done entirely on vowels that are vibrations. Consonants are also vibrations, partially stopped or entirely stopped by the lips, teeth, tongue, or palate. The great problem in singing is to keep the vowels flowing and have as little interference as possible from the consonants. The only consonant sounds that are really difficult for the singer are the consonants p and t and k, because there the stoppage is entire because these sounds are noises. Since the consonants make the drama in music, and since drama is in large part portrayal of mood, consonants seem to come naturally into their right place in the musical line if we do not become too technical in their study. In other words, if we can continually keep the creation of a beautiful line as a creative faculty and not a technical study, it is possible for a conductor as a creative human being quickly to lead his choir and his singers into the realms of creative power. We train animals to remember; human beings must create. Our music must be used to inspire our listeners and to lift them above the realm of commonplace, everyday life. If each one of us finds a way to become creative, and at the same time to obey laws, life can be a happy experience for us.

My Career

Mrs. John Finley Williamson, class of 1911, (Rhea Parlette) received the Otterbein "Woman of the Year" award at the annual dinner meeting of the Westerville Otterbein Women's Club on Saturday February 17, 1962
Mrs. Williamson served as Dean of the Westminster Choir College, Princeton, New Jersey, from the time of its founding by her husband, Dr. John Finley Williamson, until their retirement in 1960. In 1951, Otterbein College conferred the honorary degree of Doctor of Humane Letters upon Mrs. Williamson. This is the text of her speech.

by Mrs. John Finley Williamson (Rhea Parlette)

Speech at Otterbein College, February 1962

Indeed I have no words adequate to express my gratitude to you for the honor you are bestowing upon me today. I'm certain that through the years you have honored many far more worthy than I, but never have honored anyone more inwardly grateful than I.

I love Otterbein, I have always loved her. I have never needed to apologize for her. As we look back over a span of years we are prone to think, "If I had my life to live over again, I'd do so and so." There are two areas at least where I would do exactly the same thing over again—in spite of what scholarships might await me, I'd come back to Otterbein and I'd marry my dear Jack, who sends his greetings to you from Canton, Ohio, where he is recovering from a slight heart attack.

What a time I attended Otterbein 1907-1911. Imagine any small college having on its faculty at one time a Dr. Miller, a Dr. Scott, a Dr. Scanders, a Professor Wagner and a Dr. Roselot. Oh with what admiration I remember these men—how I cried over those problems of Dr. Miller's that just wouldn't come out right until he with a touch of magic did them on the black board so simply. Dr. Scott's shaking forefinger, that with a sudden thrust and a glance over his glasses made you know that the floor was yours! Prof. Wagner's look in the opposite direction as he announced "Rhea Beatrice Parlette, 2402 South Wayne Ave. Dayton, Ohio." What a man for statistics and what a memory. Oh, yes, he required that we memorize to writing and punctuating perfection the opening lines of Caesar. I still feel grateful to him for this as our grandchildren are struggling with Caesar and I nonchalantly after fifty years start repeating, "Galliae est omnes divisea in partes tres." Bobbie was bewildered, his eyes opened wider and wider and when I came to the end of Prof. Wagner's requirement he gasped, "Nanna you know everything don't you"! Not often one gets such a compliment!

And how well I remember Dr. Sanders after a class saying, "I should like to see you at 3:00 this afternoon." "What had I done"? Well, I found out. Dr. Sanders seated me courteously, then said, "I see you passing my home very frequently with that Williamson young man. I just wondered if you realized you are getting very serious." I looked him squarely in the eye and said, "Oh yes, Dr. Sanders, I love him." Dr. Sanders patted me on the arm and said, "That's all right my dear, that's all that matters." And after having been married 50 years this coming June, I reiterate, "That's all that has mattered."

The only distinguished thing I ever did was to marry Jack. While he was in Otterbein, some of you may remember that he was allergic to academic work, but he sang beautifully and left here with nothing more than a diploma in voice. The only thing he knew was to teach voice, so he opened a studio. I realize some of you are thinking—it's your career not his we wish to know about. I have no way of separating them. Several years ago Temple University, Philadelphia, gave us each a doctor's degree citing us as a husband and wife team in education, and so we have remained through the years.

Somehow Jack had an inner ear for music and quickly developed a church choir to such a degree of excellence that a New York manager contracted to take it on tour—this at a time when churches were served by quartets not choirs. Imagine if you can on that first tour our singing in Carnegie Hall, New York; Symphony Hall, Boston; Academy of Music, Philadelphia; and being reviewed by the best music critics in the country. Whether we liked it or not we were literally shoved into our career. It seemed that every minister, who heard the choir sing wanted someone to similarly train his young people, and out of demand in 1926 we founded Westminster Choir

College in Dayton, Ohio. What did Jack know about courses, credits, state accreditation, etc. and what did I know about music—absolutely nothing! By joining forces—Jack as president and I as dean and teacher of the English courses—we got along. I believe God gave us ability we didn't have and because our College was dedicated to the service of the church we attracted fine young people, who in time graduated and were placed in churches across the country and in mission fields around the world. As teachers went, students came.

When the College was three years old, through the influence of Mrs. H.E. Talbott, who for years was our devoted sponsor of Westminster Choir, President Hoover sent us on tour through Europe. Fortunately, I, on this tour, as on all later tours, was to take care of protocol and all the niceties and social aspects of such a tour, which meant that I had to attend teas and receptions and sit in the royal boxes.

Our first concert on that tour was in Bristol, England, from whence our ancestors sailed for this country years ago. This was a preliminary concert before our big night in London. I recall yet the nervous tension of that day with its morning rehearsal and final admonitions. My husband threatened the young people thus, "If any one of you forgets anything when we leave for Bristol this afternoon I have right here in my pocket a return ticket that will take you back to the U.S. Of course, I knew he hadn't as he swept his hand over his pocket, but here we were in the recognized choral country of the world—young, inexperienced, and scared. In due time, we arrived at the concert hall. Jack was taken to his dressing room with a boy to help him dress. I sat outside spiteless and motionless. Finally I became alarmed when I saw this boy rush out three times, ignoring me each time. So as he went out, I went in. There stood Jack in full evening dress except for his pants, which he had forgotten. The trips that the boy made were to exchange Jack's gray pants for dark ones. So, he directed this first concert in an usher's pants and did he go home the next day? Emphatically no! That tour was a success. We sang in the Queen's Hall and in the great Albert Hall. In Paris, ours was the first concert other than Opera in that hallowed Paris Opera House. The President, his wife, and the government officials were in attendance. It was thrilling when they stood with us as we closed our program with "The Star Spangled Banner" and thus we sang in all the countries of Europe. In the Vienna Opera House, only Fritz Kreisler and Westminster Choir had given concerts other than opera.

When we returned we had chosen Princeton, New Jersey, as our permanent college home, first because my husband felt that unless we could live within commuting distance of New York City and unless he could make his choir good enough to sing with the Philharmonic Orchestra he had not reached his goal and second because our dear Dr. Charles R. Erdman, then Moderator of the Presbyterian Church lived in Princeton and had somehow arranged that our little college receive an invitation to locate in Princeton from the President of Princeton University, President of Princeton Seminary, and the Governor of New Jersey.

And so our college grew. Additional students came and additional demands for our graduates came.

During the years Jack's goal—fantastic as it seemed, was realized and Westminster College Choir sang 146 concerts with the Philharmonic Orchestra in Carnegie Hall, New York, under such great men as John Barbaroli, Leopold Stokowski, Toscanini, Rachmaninoff, Bruno Walter, Metropolis, Rodjinski, Ormandy, Cantelli, and Bernstein. Jack says proudly, "I studied scores with these men," while I say, "I dined these men."

One time when Mr. Toscanini came for a rehearsal, Jack had to be in North Carolina for a festival, so when the rehearsal was over I gave him Jack's greeting and regrets that he could not be there to take him home for lunch. Mr. Toscanini with one of his quick gestures said, "Is there any reason I can't go home with you"? I quickly recovered myself and said, "Why no, I didn't know you'd care to." "Well, I do," he said and after lunch he talked to me three hours about his life in Italy.

Then in 1934 just after our country had recognized Russia, President Roosevelt sent us to Russia. Their revolution had liquidated thousands of white Russians and left largely the serfs in power. They wore no personal adornment—jewelry, fancy buttons, scarfs, or anything. Office workers looked like cleaning people. We were then sharing some of our best scientists with them. They knew no techniques. What they have accomplished since is amazing. We saw Stalin, but were never received by him. We sang their International at the beginning of our program and our "Star Spangled Banner" at the close. They loved our choir—clapped, stamped, stood, and shouted.

Dictatorship was evidenced at every turn, but even at that these people were having it so much better than under the Czar that no one objected. We viewed Lenin in the tomb from which Kruschev removed the body of Stalin a few weeks ago. If this is the embalmed body of Lenin, it represents the most perfect embalming imaginable.

In the meantime things were happening at home in a way that was almost miraculous. The Princeton churches housed our College after we moved to Princeton, their organs and pianos were used for teaching and practice and their rooms for classes.

At the Seminary Commencement for which our choir sang, Mrs. Sophia Taylor, of Cleveland, Ohio sat next to me and asked me if Jack and I would have dinner with her that evening at the Princeton Inn. We had met her only once before briefly, but she liked the way our choir was received and had listened weekly to our broadcasts with Mr. Walter Damrosch. We met her at the Inn, were seated and served our soup course when she said, "I want to give you four hundred thousand dollars with which to build your college building"—and this in the heart of the depression with banks closed and bread lines everywhere." Then she added, "I want to give it to you tonight. I have a heart that may take me to my glory anytime." Well, we called the presidents of the two banks, every real estate man in town, who came hurrying. We went about with flashlights looking at this and that site, however nothing was decided until summer. Here we were from May until mid-summer with nothing to prove a thing so fantastic could happen to us. I have always felt so grateful that Mrs. Taylor lived to visit school and to get acquainted with the students. Here some of the greatest musicians of our day have visited us in our Colonial style buildings of Virginia brick and Vermont marble.

In 1956 Mr. Eisenhower confronted Jack with an invitation to take his choir on a trip around the world. This we did. We set out from International Airport, San Francisco with passports, shot cards, and many don'ts as to eating and drinking. I wish I could review these countries. We sang before native groups and found all people kind and responsive. In India we walked along those Bazaar streets rubbing elbows with the cold slimy noses of the sacred cows, whose rights were far greater than ours. One day I was tugging along in the crowd,

93

unconsciously keeping step with what I thought was a cow. I looked up and still up to see it was a camel that had singled me out.

Before the entrance of our fine hotels were cows giving a barn yard aspect to the entrance, but what bothered me more was the possibility of stepping on a human being, one of the three and a half million who sleep every night on the ground in India.

What a sight was the Sacred Ganges—all things to all people— some washing their meager wearing apparel, some baring their bodies for cleansing, some cupping their hands and sipping the water in ceremonial rites, some using the river for sewerage purposes and yet some for throwing in the remaining unburned portions of those bodies wrapped in muslin and thrown on the funeral pyres. How distressing is India with her seething millions tramping, tramping, tramping, with no place to go and in contrast to all this misery is that breath-taking glistening Taj-Mah Hall.

A trip by plane from Japan to Korea was perhaps my most harassing experience. The craft was one of those old globe masters, carrying 100 soldiers upstairs and Westminster Choir on bucket seats around the outside edge with our baggage strapped to the floor in front of us. We wore parachutes and mae-wests. I have never been so uncomfortable and just as I was thinking, "Well, rather than jump were the signal to sound, I'd be courageous and go down with the plane," the young officer continued, "If any of you are thinking you won't jump as ordered, let me tell you, you'll be pushed out!"

In Okinawa we had the largest crowd we have ever had at a concert—20,000 young men and women, some of whom had walked seven miles to attend. We had sung in the greatest music halls of many countries, but never had we had such an audience crowded in sitting on the ground before a built-up stage for the choir. Their eagerness and attention brought tears to my eyes.

Upon our return to this country Jack received recognition from the State Department and President and Mrs. Eisenhower entertained us at the White House. It was a small party—the cabinet and their wives. Mr. Eisenhower spoke individually to each individual and made each one feel that he had served his country worthily.

The following summer Jack and I went back to Japan to teach in many schools. I had classes in drama and he in singing and conducting. He was able to eliminate that scratchy Japanese tone.

They sang beautifully and wept for joy when they listened to each other. One Japanese school asked me to give the opening talk. After that it became my mission to speak from morning until night in most of the schools in Tokyo. I shall always keep in mind a beautiful picture. I was seated with the principal on the stage before several hundred girls in maroon uniforms and as I stood before the podium simultaneously those girls with nary a blonde among them bowed. It reminded me of the wind passing over a wheat field. Everyone bows in Japan. I always told Jack that when we found ourselves bowing to each other when we got up in the morning, it was time for us to leave Japan.

Our teaching carried us on to Honolulu, Hong Kong (in my mind the most interesting city in the world), to Thailand where I gave a play with two interpreters. Here for the first time we entered a leprosy colony and taught these most cheerful grateful people.

Last year we again left the States August 3, to return April 15, we had classes in eight far Eastern countries and in New Zealand. When we got to the Southern tip of New Zealand, I noticed a sign 2,249 miles to the South Pole. I loved New Zealand, although I couldn't happily exchange our beautiful dipper for their Southern Cross. With shadows falling on the wrong side and a strange aspect of the Heavens I felt thousands of miles away from home. However, after six months of Oriental food, always eaten with chopsticks and after speaking every word through an interpreter, there was something restful about New Zealand. Jack had numerous classes and choirs and I got to lecture in their largest university on Drama.

In Bangkok, Jack was commissioned by the King to give four performances of Handel's Messiah with the King's Royal Thai Orchestra accompanying—one in each of the two large universities, on in the Chinese church, and one in the Christian Church. We felt very happy about this since before our first visit with the choir Jack was greeted by the Thai Ambassador in Washington, told that his King welcomed him to Thailand, but that he wished no Christian music, that 97% of his people were Buddhists and desired to stay that way. Jack asked if the classics and Negro Spirituals would do. "Oh yes," was the reply, so Westminster Choir sang throughout Thailand, "Steal Away to Jesus," "Were You There," and the like. And now to be commissioned by the King to sing the Messiah with native singers and the Royal Orchestra was pleasing. There were beautiful programs with all the words done in both Thai and English, but at the top of the program was this line, "A Secular Rendition of Handel's Messiah."

Between these two teaching missions a couple of very important things happened to us.

In 1958 at the age of 70, we retired from our dear Westminster Choir College. How can people look forward to retirement!

But almost at that very moment President Eisenhower invited us to take a choir on tour throughout Africa. We had plenty to think about during the next few weeks—choosing a choir of former graduates, making up programs, choosing hot climate costumes, etc. However, on New Year's Day they dropped out of the Heavens from North, South, East, and West for their training period. Two intensive weeks of preparation and we were off across the Atlantic.

Our first concert was in Dakar on the West Coast of Africa. But the next day a very wonderful thing happened. In Freetown, Sierre Leone, the mountains rise too close to the shore for the planes to land, so the landing strip is built out into the ocean. We went into shore on a barge. As we came into dock, I heard distinctly, "Otterbein! Otterbein!" I was so surprised that I answered almost unconsciously, "Otterbein." I hadn't known that Dr. John Kareefus Smart was there and that we were to be his house guests while there. Oh yes, where we might have a pet cat they have a pet monkey. He was your Commencement Speaker last Commencement and what a man of influence he is in his own country.

Since Africa is so much in the news just now, I must give a few details: How right Cecil Rhodes was when he said, "In Africa think big."

The country is four times the size of the U.S. Its Nile River is the longest river in the world. The second largest lake in the world is in Africa. The Congo River some places widens to nine miles. The mist and roar which David Livingston followed down the Zambesi River turned out to be Victoria Falls, 1 mile wide, 1-1/2 times wider and twice as high as Niagara Falls. The Zambesi River flows 800 miles, then leaps 355 feet and carves out a narrow gorge to the Indian Ocean 900 miles away.

We visited the Firestone Plantations—86,000 acres, 30,000 workers who earn $0.44 a day. The trees are planted in rows for miles and miles and tapped as our Maple trees are. This milky substance is packed in bales and shipped off to make our Firestone Tires.

After having our passports held for more than a week we were admitted to the diamond mines. This is a real prison enclosure, the men are hired on a seven-month term and never leave the enclosure during that time. The diamonds are in the surface soil and look like bits of camphor ice. The Big Hole as it is known stands near by partially filled with water. It is a silent reminder of the excavations from 1871 to 1914 which gave forth three tons of diamonds.

In Germiston 3-1/2 million pounds of gold bullion are taken out each week. Great mounds of yellow slag bear evidence. It is true, Africa does not belong to the Black Man. Segregation is a problem there and surely there is reason for the trouble reported currently in the newspapers. Free men and slaves cannot live in the same society.

Night after night we sang in this very rich Africa, sometimes to well-educated Oxford and Cambridge graduates. (England sent many blacks back to England to be educated). Sometimes to those from the Jungles, one (removed) generation removed from cannibalism, sometimes before naked children and women dressed in skirts only. Jack taught children and adults after the concerts were over, to sing with the choir, "Oh What a Beautiful Morning, Oh What a Beautiful Day" and everyone left feeling a joyous oneness with each other.

We sang for the Watusies, 7 feet tall and perhaps at the same concert to the pygmies 4 feet tall.

What an experience in a country made up of 20,000 whites and 140,000,000 blacks, with modern cities, four great universities with few students, and such natural resources.

We sang to 202,000 persons of various races and nationalities. And on last year's teaching mission we had 18,204 in our classes—our conclusion, all people are wonderful; the color of skin is non consequential when the heart speaks.

Now with being a wife, mother, and grandmother, and great-grandmother, this is my career. Call it what you will, but I thank God for every day of it.

Our next assignment is to set up the first school of Sacred Music in Japan in 1963.

****

Joseph G. Beck

Men are tattooed with their special beliefs like so many South Sea Islanders; but a real human heart with divine love in it beats with the same glow under all the patterns of all earth's thousand tribes.

-Oliver Wendell Holmes-

****

A Singer's Guide to Diction in the English Language

from lectures and writings by John Finley Williamson

Collected and Revised by Joseph G. Beck edited by Heather M. Wessels

Vowels

Tones are sustained on the vowel sounds.

Fundamentals	Medial	Subordinates
soon	task	soot
sew		sod
saw		sung
psalm		sat
say		set
see		sit

Singing Vowels:
- When the vowel "a" is followed by two consonants, it always has the medial "ah" sound, as in "task."
- All vowels in unaccented syllables have the sound of "uh," as in "sung," with a tinge of the vowel that is present.
- Articles preceding words with initial consonants are short ("a day," "thə day"); articles preceding words with initial vowels (or vowel sounds) are long ("an hour," "an apple," "the hour," "the apple").

Diphthongs

Analysis of Diphthongs:
   A diphthong is a sound made up of two vowels, one sustained and the other treated as a vanishing vowel.

Diphthong (example)	Sustained Vowel (as in)	Vanishing Vowel (as in)
vow	psalm	soon
vie	psalm	see
voice	sung	see
view*	see	soon
say	set	see
so	rose	soon

*sustained and vanished vowels are reversed for this diphthong

Singing Diphthongs:
   • The vanishing vowel of a diphthong is given the same time value as a consonant.
   • The vowel "u" is treated as the diphthong in "view" when it follows "t" ("Tuesday"), "d" ("dew"), "n" ("news"), "s" ("assume"), "p" ("pure"), and "m" ("music").

Consonants

A consonant is the vibration of the vocal cords partially or entirely stopped by the lips, teeth, tongue, or palate.

Vocal Consonants Having Pitch

m
n
l
r
v
z   (as in "**z**ebra")
zh   (as in "a**z**ure," "vi**s**ion," or "plea**s**ure")
th   (as in "**th**ee")
ng   (as in "si**ng**")
w
y
b   (sub-vocal at beginning of word)

Consonants Without Pitch

Voiced Explosive Consonants	Pure Explosive Consonants
• b (voiced at end of word) • d • g • j (as in "**judge**")	• p (made with the lips) • t (made with the tip of tongue) • k (made with the back of tongue)

Joseph G. Beck

Sibilants (a high frequency noise)	**Aspirates** (a puff of breath)
• f (as in "**f**ood") • s (a single final "s" has the sound of "z," as in "ha**s**," also, "s" between two vowels frequently sounds as "z" as in "rea**s**on" and "no**s**e" and when indicating possessives and plurals as in "the boy'**s** dog**s**") • sh (as in "**sh**oe") • ch (as in "**ch**urch") • th (as in "**th**ink")	• h (as in "**h**ope") • wh (as in "**wh**ich") **Lip Consonants** • m (as in "**m**ary") • b (as in "**b**ought") • p (as in "**p**arsnips") • f (as in "**f**or") • v (as in "**v**egetables")

Singing Consonants:

- Consonants having pitch must be sung on the same pitch as the vowel that follows.
- All consonants made with the tip or back of the tongue demand a quiet jaw and an active tongue.
- All explosive consonants should be separated from the vowel that follows (as in "**c**ome").
- Voiced explosive consonants have the sound of "uh" at the end of a word (as in "**G**od").
- The time value of the consonant depends on the drama of the word.
- When one word ends and the next begins with the same consonant, only one consonant is sounded, unless the sounding of both heightens the dramatic effect. If the consonant has pitch and the words are on two different pitches, both consonants are articulated.
- "B" at the beginning of a word is a sub-vocal consonant having pitch; at the end of a word "b" is a voiced explosive only.
- When a nasal consonant ("n" or "ng") at the end of a word is above the pitch C (for basses, baritones, and altos) and above pitch E (for tenors and sopranos), it is treated as a voiced consonant.
- The consonant "r":
  i. preceding a vowel in a word denoting action can be rolled.
  ii. preceding a vowel in a word not denoting action is burred or flipped (as in "th**r**ee").
  iii. when a word ends in the unaccented syllable of "er," "or," or "ar," the consonant "r" has the sound of "uh" as in "sung" and is sustained (as in "fath**er**").
  iv. when the consonant "r" follows a vowel, a diphthong, or a triphthong, it becomes a vanishing vowel of a diphthong, triphthong ("h**our**"), or a quadthong ("ch**oir**"), and has the vanishing sound of "uh" as in "sung."

Singing "Or"

I. "Or" is often pronounced as a diphthong:

A. When "or" is used as a word itself, or comes at the beginning of a word on an accented syllable which precedes a consonant (as in "**ord**er," "**orph**an," "**orn**ament"), it is a diphthong, having the sustained sound of "aw" (as in "s**aw**") and the vanishing sound of "uh" (as in "s**ung**").

B. "Or" is a diphthong having the sustained sound of "aw" (as in "saw") and the vanishing sound of "uh" (as in "sung") when:

1. the "or" is followed by a silent "e" (as in "ad**ore**," "y**ore**," "m**ore**," "sh**ore**," "bef**ore**").

2. when "or" is combined with other silent vowels (as in "b**oar**d," "m**our**n," "fl**oor**").

3. the dictionary pronunciation indicates the long sound of "o" (as in "sp**ort**," "w**orn**," "f**ord**")

C. At the end of a word, when "or follows a vowel (as in "met**eor**"), or an aspirate (as in "ab**hor**"), it is a diphthong having the sustained sound of "aw" (as in "s**aw**)" and the vanishing sound of "uh" (as in "s**ung**").

II. "Or" can have the single vowel sound of "uh" (as in "sung"):

A. Although the dictionary indicates that "or" following "w" (as in "**wor**d," "**wor**k," "**wor**ld," "**wor**ship," "**wor**th") is pronounced in spoken English with the same sound as the "u" in "**u**rge" and the "ea" in "**ea**rth," the pronunciation when sung is different. When reducing all sounds to fundamentals for choir purposes, "or" following "w" has the sound of "uh" as in "s**ung**." For the soloist, there should be a tinge of the "r" present.

104

B. At the end of a word, when there is an unaccented syllable following a consonant (as in "honor"), it has the single vowel sound of "uh" as in "s**u**ng."

III. "Or" can have the single vowel sound of "aw" (as in "s**aw**"):

A. In the middle of a word, when "or" precedes a consonant in words whose dictionary pronunciation indicates the short sound of "o" (as in "**north**," "**Lord**," "**fort**ress," "**born**," "**horse**," "**forg**et"), it has the single vowel sound of "aw" (as in "saw").

B. When "or" is found at the beginning of a word on an unaccented syllable which precedes a consonant (as in "**ord**ain" and "**orn**ate"), or on a syllable with a secondary accent (as in "**or**chestration" and "**or**dination"), it has the single vowel sound of "aw" (as in "s**aw**").

C. When "or" precedes a vowel at the beginning or in the middle of a word (as in "gl**ory**," "**ori**ent," "**ora**tor," "st**ory**"), the vowel has the sound of "aw" (as in "s**aw**") and the "r" is burred.

IV. "Or" can also have the sound of "o" as in "sod":

A. When "or" is followed by a second "r" and a vowel (as in "tom**orro**w," "**sorro**w," "**borro**w"), it has the single vowel sound as in "sod," and the second "r" is burred.

Westminster Choir: Recordings as History and Discography

by Joseph G. Beck

Editor's Note: The text of the following article and discography originally appeared in the November 1976 issue of the *Choral Journal* and was reprinted in the 1996 November issue. The discography that concluded these articles has been updated to include recordings through the year 2001.

The year 1976 marked the fiftieth anniversary of the Westminster Choir College and the Westminster Choir from which the College takes its name. In Dayton, Ohio, at the Westminster Presbyterian Church, a young choral director, John Finley Williamson , created what is now called the famous Westminster Choir for the music program of that church. Williamson became Director of Music at the church in 1920 and proceeded to build an outstanding choir. Many of America's prominent choral directors, including Peter Lutkin and F. Melius Christiansen, encouraged Williamson and helped him with his early tours. In 1926 the Dayton Westminster Choir became the Westminster Choir School (later college) and three years later awarded diplomas to its first graduates. The school was designed to train men and women to serve as ministers of music in the Protestant Church and to train people for teaching in schools and colleges.

As a student of Herbert Witherspoon and David Bispham, two of America's outstanding singers and voice teachers, Williamson was a knowledgeable vocalist and treated his rehearsals as a voice class. Using laws of acoustics as a basis for his choral sound, he stressed the vitality of tone that he considered essential to good singing. Because of his many radio broadcasts with the Westminster Choir during the 1930s, (also with the New York Philharmonic and other major symphony orchestras), Williamson's influence on American choral music has been significant and far-reaching.

The object of the paper, however, is not primarily to give a history of Westminster Choir College or its choir. It is to trace the development of this choral tradition by examining the large output of records over a [seventy five-year] span. To show the development of this tradition, all the discussions in this article are based on the accompanying discography. Most of the records listed are available for scholars at Westminster Choir College and are housed there as part of the Talbott Library-Learning Center.

The Westminster "tone" can be traced from the choir's earliest recording (Victor #20410, (1926) of Lotti's *Crucifixus* and Palestrina's *Hodie Christus natus est*. The tonal quality of the choir is flute-like and has very little vibrato. This shows an influence of the St. Olaf and the northwestern a cappella choirs. After the Westminster choir's first European tour in 1929, it developed more sophisticated choral phrasing due to Williamson's direct contact with the choral tradition of Europe.

Shortly after the European tour in 1929, the choir school outgrew its home in Dayton and moved to Ithaca, New York, to become part of the Ithaca Conservatory of Music; Williamson served as dean. In 1932, when the opportunity was presented for the choir to take up a permanent home in Princeton, New Jersey, Williamson's life-long dream of performing with the country's major symphony orchestras was to be realized.

During this period, primarily due to the Great Depression, no recordings were made; however, Westminster Choir continued its tours throughout the U.S. In the fall of 1934, the choir traveled once again to Europe and spent over two months in Russia. In December of that year, the choir sang with a major orchestra for the first time. They performed Bach's *B-Minor Mass* with the Philadelphia Orchestra conducted by Leopold Stokowski. The 1936 recording of Bach's motet for double choir *Sing Ye to the Lord* (Victor #1845 and #14613) illustrates a departure from the earlier tone quality. The tone is darker, has a richer quality, and shows the influence of the Russian style of choral singing, especially with the great emphasis on the bass section.

The Roy Harris recording, *When Johnny Comes Marching Home*, released in 1938 (Victor #1883), shows a much more sophisticated style of singing. This growing sophistication was due in part to the influence of Williamson's work with symphony orchestras. The choir's first performance with the New York Philharmonic was conducted by Sir John Barbirolli in 1937. From that date on, the Westminster Choir performed regularly with the New York Philharmonic under such conductors as Toscanini, Walter, Bernstein, and many others. In 1940, Westminster Choir began to record for Columbia Records.

The first recording with symphony orchestra was the Brahms *Schicksalslied* (Columbia set X233), conducted by Bruno Walter and recorded in the early 1940s. The tonal quality of the recordings made from the early 1940s through 1958, when Williamson retired, all have the characteristic "Westminster sound." There were slight fluctuations with either a darkening or lightening of tone, as Williamson seemed to love to experiment. However, the tone quality was always very vibrant and rich (especially the men's voices), which was a characteristic of his work.

The 1950s ushered in the long-playing record, and with this innovation came better fidelity. Probably the most beautiful recording from this era was the Mozart *Requiem* (Columbia ML 5012). Williamson told me that he thought it was one of the finest examples of his choral concept and the best reproduction of the sound. The women's tone is much more lyric, as in the very early recordings of Westminster Choir. Williamson's concepts seemed to go full circle. As he progressed, he experimented with many different types of tonal production and qualities. In his last recordings the soprano and alto voices again became more lyric; however, they never lost that vibrant sound and "ring."

Following the move to Princeton, the term "Westminster Choir" could mean any number of the college's several choirs. The Westminster (Touring) Choir was composed of forty select voices. The Symphonic Choir included upper class students and performed with major symphonies. The choir's size for recordings with orchestra varied according to the literature performed, e.g., Messiah was recorded with some fifty singers, the *Ninth Symphony* with approximately 150.

After Williamson retired in 1958, Warren Martin, a Westminster Choir College graduate, conducted the Westminster Choir for several years and retained some elements of the characteristic Westminster tone. The Beethoven *Missa solemnis* of 1962 (Columbia MAS619) exemplified this era. From 1964 to 1968, George Lynn, another graduate and disciple of Williamson, was conductor of the Westminster Choir, and the 1966 recording of Verdi's *Requiem* (Columbia M2S707) has a more characteristic Williamson sound. From 1969 to 1972, Westminster Choir was conducted by various conductors including Elaine Brown and Robert Carwithen. The current conductor is Joseph Flummerfelt, a student of Robert Shaw and Elaine Brown. His recordings are a departure from the so-called "Westminster Sound." The recording of Haydn's *Mass in B^b* (Columbia M-33267) is an example of his choral concepts.

The noncommercial recordings listed in the discography are primarily those of the Toscanini Society. They show Westminster Choir as it was during the years before the Second World War. The recordings were made from "air checks" before broadcasts of the New York Philharmonic during the late 1930s and early 1940s. Although the recordings do not have good fidelity, they do give some insight to the quality and sound of Westminster Choir during that era. Westminster Choir, beginning with its founder and first conductor, John Finley Williamson, and through it subsequent directors—Warren Martin, George Lynn, Elaine Brown, and Joseph Flummerfelt—has changed but still exerts a strong influence on choral music in America and the world.

Westminster Choir Discography 1926-2001

Key to Abbreviations
*   78 r.p.m.
LP   long playing mono
LPS   stereo
LPES   electronically processed stereo
CAS   cassette
CD   compact disc
date   date of issue
(All listed long playing records are 12")
The commercial recordings are listed in approximate order of issue. In most cases the release date of the commercial recordings is within a year of the recording date. Exact recording dates have been included where they can be determined.

1926

Palestrina—*Hodie Christus natus est*
Lotti—*Crucifixus*
Dayton Westminster Choir, Williamson
10" Victor 20410*
10" Electrola EG 136*
10" HMV D1647*

1928

Gilbert Alcock—*Celestial Voices*
Marsh—*Jesus Lover of My Soul*
Dayton Westminster Choir, Williamson
10" Victor 20468*
10" HMV B2986*

1929
Palestrina—*Hodie Christus natus est*
Kolsolyoff—*Alleluia Christ is Risen*
Gilbert Alcock—*Celestial Voices*
Dayton Westminster Choir, Williamson
10" HMV E535*
10" Electrola EW65*

Palestrina—*Exsultate Deo*
Dvorak—*Goin' Home*
Lotti—*Crucifixus*
Dayton Westminster Choir, Williamson
12" HMV D1647*
12" Electrola EJ430*

Palestrina—*Exaltabo te, Domine*
Nicholsky—*O Praise Ye the Name of the Lord*
Tschesnokoff [sic]—*Salvation is Created*
Dayton Westminster Choir, Williamson
12" British Columbia LXC21*

c. 1930s
Christiansen—*Beautiful Savior* (arr.)
Westminster Choir, Williamson
12" RCA CS 92172*

1936
Bach—*Motet for Double Choir*
Westminster Choir, Williamson
Sing Ye to the Lord—1st movement
10" Victor 1845*
Like as a Father—2nd movement
12" Victor 14713*
Praise Ye the Lord—3rd movement

1937
Roy Harris—*Symphony for Voices*
Westminster Choir, Williamson
2-12" RCA Victor Red Seal 14803*, 14804*
Set: Musical Masterpiece Series M427*

1938
Roy Harris—*When Johnny Comes Marching Home*
Spiritual—*Water Boy*
Westminster Choir, Williamson
10" Victor 1883*

Beethoven—*Symphony No. 9 in D minor*, Op. 125
NBC Symphony Orchestra, Toscanini; Bovy, Thorborg, Peerce, Pinza
Westminster Choir, Williamson
5-10" Victor 18846-18850
- Reissued (1988) on **Toscanini Conducts Beethoven** as Music & Arts CD 3007
- Reissued (1999) as LYS 408 CD

1939
Rossini—*Petite Messe Solennelle*
New York Philharmonic, Barbirolli
Westminster Choir, Williamson
Carnegie Hall Recording Co. [not commercial] 19 sides, 10"

1941
Roy Harris—*Songs for Occupations*
Westminster Choir, Williamson
12" Columbia 68347*, 68348*, set M227*

Earl Robinson—*Ballad for Americans*
John Baumgartner and Westminster Choir, Williamson
2-10" Columbia set C49*

1942

Choral Christmas Music: *O Come All Ye Faithful; Silent Night*
Westminster Choir, Williamson
10" Columbia 5509*

Choral Christmas Music: *Serbian Crib Carol; Joseph Came Seeking a Resting Place; Song of the Christmas Presents*
Westminster Choir, Williamson
12" Columbia 17351-D*
  • Reissued (1997) on **Heritage the Christmas Album: Holiday Melodies** as Sony Classical MHK 63309

Choral Christmas Music: *Carillon; Carol of the Bells*
Westminster Choir, Williamson
10" Columbia 36419*

Choral Christmas Music: *The Song of Mary; Sing We All Nowell*
Westminster Choir, Williamson
10" Columbia 36420*

1943

Bach—*St. Matthew Passion*
New York Philharmonic, Walter; Conner, Watson, Hain, Alvary, Harrell, Janssen
Westminster Choir, Williamson
Carnegie Hall Recording Co. [not commercial] 28 sides, 10"
  • Reissued (1989) as AS Disc (Europe) AS 406

1944

Brahms—*Schicksalslied (Song of Destiny)*, Op. 54
New York Philharmonic, Walter
Westminster Choir, Williamson
O Heilland, Reiss' die Himmel auf (O Savior Throw the Heavens Wide)
Westminster Choir, Williamson
2-12" Columbia X-233*

- Reissued (1949) with Beethoven's *Symphony No. 9* as 2- Columbia SL156 LP

Walton—*Belshazzar's Feast*
New York Philharmonic, Rodzinski; Brownlee
Westminster Choir, Williamson
with Elgar *Pomp and Circumstance*
Carnegie Hall Recording Co. [not commercial] 8 sides, 10"

1945

Prokofiev—*Alexander Nevsky*, Op. 78
Philadelphia Orchestra, Ormandy; Tourel
Westminster Choir, Williamson
5-12" Columbia 12156/60*, set MM580*
British Columbia X977/81*
Cantoria (France) 15877/81*, set D141*
(in English and Latin)

- Reissued (1949) as Columbia ML4247 LP

Beethoven—*Symphony No. 9 in D minor*, Op. 125
Philadelphia Orchestra, Ormandy; Roma, Szantho, Jagel, Moscona
Westminster Choir, Williamson
8-12" Columbia set M591*

- Reissued as 2-12" Columbia set SL150 LP

Foss—*The Prairie*
New York Philharmonic, Rodzinski
Westminster Choir, Williamson
Carnegie Hall Recording Co. 13 sides [not commercial] 10"

c. 1948
Golden Anniverary Album: Hymns of the Month 1948-1949
National Federation of Music Clubs
Westminster Choir, Williamson; Morrisey
10" Westminster Choir College WC 101-109

1949
Beethoven—*Symphony No. 9* and Brahms—*Schickasalslied*
New York Philharmonic, Walter; Gonzalez, Nikolaidi, Jobin, Harrell
Westminster Choir, Williamson
8-12" Columbia set MM-900*
2-Columbia SL156 LP

1953
Beethoven—*Symphonies No. 9 and No. 8*
New York Philharmonic, Walter; Yeend, Lipton, Lloyd, Harrell
Westminster Choir, Williamson
2-12" Columbia set ML186 LP
- Reissued (1957) with *Symphony No. 9* only as Columbia ML5200
- Reissued (1967) as Odyssey 32160322 LP
- Reissued (1969) on **Complete Beethoven Symphonies** as Odyssey 3266001 LPS

1955
Bruckner—*Te Deum in C, WAB 45*
with Mahler *Kindertotenlieder*, Vienna Philharmonic, Kathleen Ferrier
New York Philharmonic, Walter; Yeend, Lipton, Lloyd, Harrell
Westminster Choir, Williamson
(Recorded March 1953)
Columbia ML-4980 LP
- Reissued with Mozart's *Requiem* (1995) as Sony Classical 64480 CD

1956

Mozart—*Requiem in D minor, K 626*
New York Philharmonic, Walter; Seefried, Tourel, Simoneau, Warfield
Westminster Choir, Williamson
Columbia ML-5012 LP

- Reissued (1977) as Odyssey 34619 LP
- Reissued (1991) on **Mozart: Opera & Consert Arias/Requiem** as Sony Classical 47211 CD
- Reissued (1995) with Bruckner's *Te Deum* as Sony Classical 64480 CD

1957

Stravinsky—*Persephone*
New York Philharmonic, Stravinsky; Zorina, Robinson
Westminster Choir, Williamson
Columbia ML5196 LP

1958

Handel—*Messiah HWV 56*
New York Philharmonic, Bernstein; Addison, Oberlin, Lloyd, Warfield
Westminster Choir, Williamson
Recorded December 1956
2-Columbia M2L-242 LP, 2-Columbia M2S-603 LPS

- Reissued (1958) on **Christmas Music** as Columbia ML 5300 LP
- Reissued (1960) on **Christmas Music** as Columbia MS 6020 LPS
- Reissued (1959) on **Easter Music** as Columbia ML 5346 LP, Columbia MS 6041 LPS
- Reissued (1966) on **Highlights** as Columbia MS 6328 LPS
- Reissued (1983) excerpt "Hallelujah" Chorus on **Have a Special Holiday!** as CBS Special Products P3-20071
- Reissued (1983) on **CBS Great Performances series: Handel:** *Messiah* **Highlights** as CBS MY 38481 LPS
- Reissued (1997) excerpt "Hallelujah" Chorus on **Leonard Bernstein: The Joy of Christmas** as Sony Classical SFK 63303 CD
- Reissued (1997) on **CBS Great Performances series: Handel:** *Messiah* **Highlights** as Sony Classical 38481 CD, CAS
- Reissued (1998) on **Bernstein Century: Handel** *Messiah* as Sony Classical 60205 (2 CDs)

1959

Mahler—*Symphony No. 2 in C minor "Resurrection"*
New York Philharmonic, Walter; Cundari, Forrester
Westminster Choir, Williamson
Recorded 1956
2-Columbia M2L-256 LP
2-Columbia M2S-601 LPS

- Reissued (1971) as 2-Odyssey Y2-30848 LPS
- Reissued as Odyssey YT 30848 CD
- Reissued (1994) with *Symphony No. 1* as Sony Classical SM2K 64447 (2 CDs)

1960

Beethoven—*Symphonies No. 9 and No. 8*
Columbia Symphony, Walter; Cundari, Rankin, DaCosta, Wilderman
Westminster Choir, Martin
Recorded 1959
2-Columbia M2L-264 LP
2-Columbia M2S-608 LPS

- Reissued on **Complete Beethoven Symphonies** as 7-Odyssey Y7-30051 LPS
- Reissued (1991) on **Beethoven: The Complete Symphonies** as Sony Classical 48099 (6 CDs)
- Reissued (1995) as Sony Classical 64464 (CD)

1962

Beethoven—*Missa solemnis in D, Op 123*
New York Philharmonic, Bernstein; Farrell, Smith, Lewis, Borg
Westminster Choir, Martin
Recorded 1960
2-Columbia M2L-270 LP
2-Columbia M2S-619 LPS

- Reissued (1992) with *Fantasy for Piano* as Sony Classical S2K 47522 (2 CDs)

Prokofiev—*Alexander Nevsky*
New York Philharmonic, Shippers; Chookasian
Westminster Choir, Martin
Columbia ML-5706 LP
Columbia MS-6306 LPS

- Reissued (1972) as Odyssey Y31014 LPS
- Reissued (1995) on **Prokofiev Greatest Hits** as Sony Classical MLK 69249

1964

Beethoven—*Fantasia for Piano, Chorus, and Orchestra, Op. 80 "Choral Fantasy"*
New York Philharmonic, Bernstein; Serkin
Westminster Choir, Martin
with Beethoven's *Piano Concerto No. 3 in C minor, Op. 37*
Columbia ML6016 LP, Columbia MS6616 LPS

- Reissued (1966) on **Complete Beethoven Concertos**, Serkin, as 4-Columbia D4S 740 LPS
- Reissued (1969) with Beethoven's *Ninth Symphony*, Bernstein; Julliard Chorus, as 2-Columbia M2S 794 LPS
- Reissued (1983) as CBS MYK 38526 CD; CBS MYT 38526 CAS
- Reissued (1988) on **Great Performances: Beethoven Piano Concerto No. 3 and Choral Fantasy** as Sony Classical 38526 CD
- Reissued (1992) on **Leonard Bernstein: The Royal Edition, Vol. 11** with *Missa Solemnis & Choral Fantasy* and *Mass in B-flat major*, H. 22, No. 12 with London Symphony Orchestra/ Chorus as Sony Classical S2K 47522 (2 CDs)
- Reissued (1997) with Beethoven's *Ninth Symphony* as Sony Classical 63240 (2 CDs)

1965

Janacek—*Slavonic (Glagolitic) Mass*
New York Philharmonic, Bernstein; Pilarczyk, Martin, Gedda, Gaynes
Westminster Choir, Brown
Columbia ML-6137 LP, Columbia MS-6737 LPS

- Reissued (1992) as Sony Classical 47569 CD

Joseph G. Beck

1966
Verdi—*Messa da Requiem*
Philadelphia Orchestra, Ormandy; Amara, Forrester, Tucker, London
Westminster Choir, Lynn
2-Columbia M2L-307 LP
2-Columbia M2S-707 LPS

- Reissued (1978) as Odyssey YT 35230 CAS
- Reissued (1993) as Sony Classical S82K 53252 CD
- Reissued (1996), excerpt on **The Chorus: Greatest Hits** as Sony Classical 62684
- Reissued (1996), excerpt on **Lease Breakers** as Sony Classical 62628
- Reissued (1997), excerpt on **The Essential Classics Collection** as Sony Classical 62809
- Reissued (2000) as Sony Classical 707 CD

1967

Verdi —*Hymn of the Nations*, (from the OWI Film Dec.1943)
Nabucco, Act III—*Va, pensiero (Chorus of the Hebrew Slaves)*
NBC Symphony, Toscanini; Peerce
Westminster Choir, Williamson
(Recorded Jan. 31, 1943)
also includes overtures and solos
2-RCA Victor RB 16133/4 LP (released in England only)

Verdi—*Hymn of the Nations,* (from the OWI Film Dec. 1943)
Nabucco, Act III—*Va, pensiero (Chorus of the Hebrew Slaves)*
NBC Symphony, Toscanini; Peerce
Westminster Choir, Williamson
(Recorded Jan.31, 1943)
also includes Verdi's *Te Deum*, Shaw Choral (recoded 1954)
Victor LM-6041 LP

- Reissued (1968) as RCA Victrola VIC 1331 LP / VIC 1331(e) LPES
- Reissued (1990) on **Toscanini Collection, Vol. 63** as RCA Victor 60299
- Reissued (1990) on **Toscanini Collection, Vols. 56, 57, 63** as RCA Victor 60326

Brahms—*A German Requiem, Op. 45*
NBC Orchestra, Toscanini; Della Chiesa, Janssen
Westminster Choir, Williamson
(Recorded January 24, 1943)
Toscanini Society ATS 1001-1004 LP

- Reissued (1977) with Brahms: *Variations on a Theme of Handel* as Toscanini Society ATS 1003-1004
- Reissued (1995) as Gramofono (Italy) 78534 CD
- Reissued (2000) on **Great Conductors: Toscanini** as HNH International Ltd./Naxos Historical 8.110839

1970

Brubeck—*Gates of Justice*
Orback, Boatwright, Delcamp, Brubeck Trio
Westminster Choir, Carwithen
Decca DL 710175 LPS

Beethoven—*Choral Fantasy in C Minor, op. 80*
NBC Symphony Orchestra, Toscanini; Dorfmann, piano
Westminster Choir, Williamson
(Recorded December 2, 1939)
Toscanini Society ATS 1021 LP

- Reissued on **Toscanini Conducts Beethoven** as ATRA-3010 Discocorp LP
- Reissued (1987) with *Missa Solemnis* for ATRA on Music & Arts CD-259
- Reissued (1995) with *Symphony No. 9* as Grammofono 2000 (Italy) GRM 78524 CD
- Reissued (1998) on **Toscanini Edition Vol. 5: Beethoven** as Grammofono 2000 (Italy) GRM 78826/30 5 CDs
- Reissued (2000) on **Great Conductors: Toscanini** as HNH International Ltd./Naxos Historical 8.110824
- Reissued (2000) on **Toscanini Conducts Beethoven** as Grammofono 2000 (Italy) GRM 78007 5CDs

Verdi—*Requiem Mass* plus rehearsal segment
NBC Symphony Orchestra, Toscanini; Milanov, Castagna, Björling, Moscona
Westminster Choir, Williamson
(Recorded November 23, 1940)
Toscanini Society ATS 1005-009 5 Lps

- Reissued (1986) with Te Deum from *Quattro Pezzi Sacri* for ATRA on Music & Arts 240 2CDs

Beethoven—*Missa solemnis*
NBC Symphony Orchestra, Toscanini; Milanov, Castagna, Björling, Kipnis
Westminster Choir, Williamson
(Recorded December 28, 1940)
Toscanini Society 2-ATS 1023/24 LP
- Reissued (1980) with Verdi: *Requiem* as Italy: Melodram 006
- Reissued (1987) with *Choral Fantasy* for ATRA as Music & Arts CD-259
- Reissued (1996) as Grammofono 2000 (Italy) GRM 78626 CD

1972
Brahms—*A German Requiem*
New York Philharmonic, Walter; Seefried, London
Westminster Choir, Williamson
(Recorded 1954)
Odyssey Y31015 LP
- Reissued (1995) on **Bruno Walter Edition Series** as Sony Classical SMK 64469 CD

1973
Messiaen—*Le Transfiguration de Notre Seigneur Jesus Christ*
National Symphony Orchestra, Dorati; Sylvester, Aquino
Westminster Choir, Flummerfelt
London 0SA 1298 (2 LPs)
London-Decca CD

Joseph G. Beck

1974

Beethoven—*Symphony No. 9*
NBC Symphony Orchestra, Toscanini; Novtona, Thorburg, Peerce, Moscona
Westminster Choir, Williamson
(Recorded December 2, 1939)
Toscanini Society 2-ATS 1118/19 LP
Complete set of nine symphonies 7-ATS 1120 LP

- Reissued (1995) with *Choral Fantasy* as Grammofono 2000 (Italy) GRM 78524
- Reissued as Symposium (UK) 1230
- Reissued (1996) on **Arturo Toscanini, Vol. 6: Beethoven Symphony No. 9** as LYS 128 CD
- Reissued (1998) on **Toscanini Edition Vol. 5: Beethoven** as Grammofono 2000 (Italy) GRM 78826/30 5 CDs
- Reissued (2000) on **Great Conductors: Toscanini** as HNH International Ltd./Naxos Historical 8.110824
- Reissued (2000) on **Toscanini Conducts Beethoven** as Grammofono 2000 (Italy) GRM 78007 5CDs

Verdi—*Te Deum* (from *Four Sacred Pieces*)
New York Philharmonic, Cantelli
Westminster Choir, Williamson
(Recorded April 1, 1956)
with Verdi *Requiem*, Boston Symphony Orchestra, New England Conservatory Chorus
Recital Records IGI-340 (2 LPs)

1975

Haydn—*Mass No. 12 in Bb (Harmoniemesse)*
New York Philharmonic, Bernstein; Blegen, von Stade, Riegel, Estes
Westminster Choir, Flummerfelt
Columbia M-33267 LPS, CD

- Reissued (1978) as Moscow: Melodia 510-10075 LPS
- Reissued (1992) on **Leonard Bernstein: The Royal Edition Vol. 36** as Sony Classical 47560 2CDs

1977

Poulenc—*Gloria*
New York Philharmonic, Bernstein; Blegen
Westminster Choir, Flummerfelt
with Stravinsky *Symphony of Psalms*, London Symphony Orchestra,
English Bach Festival Chorus
Columbia 34551 LPS

- Reissued (1984) on **Leonard Bernstein Conducts Sacred Music** as Book-of-the-Month Records 61-7554
- Reissued (1988) with Bernstein: *Chichester Psalms* as CBS Masterworks MK 44710 CD
- Reissued (1992) on **Leonard Bernstein: The Royal Edition Vol. 41** as Sony Classical SMK 47569 CD

1978

Haydn—*Lord Nelson Mass*
New York Philharmonic, Bernstein; Blegen, Killebrew, Riegel, Estes
Westminster Choir, Flummerfelt
(Recorded 1976)
Columbia M35100 LPS

- Reissued (1984) on **Leonard Bernstein Conducts Sacred Music** as Book-of-the-Month Records 61-7554
- Reissued (1992) on **Leonard Bernstein: The Royal Edition, Vol. 37** with Paukenmesse *Symphony No. 88 in G Major* as Sony Classical SM2K 47563 CD

1978
Brahms—*The Complete Motets, Nos. 1-6*
Westminster Choir and Concerto Soloists of Philadelphia, Flummerfelt, Haasemann; Gray, Alexander, Haasemann, Faracco, Pratt
Beckwith, postiv organ
Westminster Recordings Division WC-1/2 LPS
- Reissued (1992) as Gothic Records G 49052 CD

Wagner—*Das Liebesmahl der Apostel* and *Siegfried Idyll*
New York Philharmonic, Boulez
Westminster Symphonic Choir, Flummerfelt
Columbia M-35131 LPS

1979
Christmas with the Westminster Choir
Westminster Choir and Concerto Soloists of Philadelphia, Flummerfelt
Beckwith, organist
Westminster Recordings Division WC 3 LP
- Reissued (1997) as Gothic Records 49047 CD, CAS

Christmas Masterpieces and Familiar Carols
- Westminster Choir, Members of the Concerto Soloists of Philadelphia, and New Jersey Symphony, Flummerfelt
- Gothic Records G 47931

- Mahler—*Symphony No. 3 in D minor*
- New York Philharmonic, Mitropoulos; Krebs
- Westminster Choir, Williamson
- (Recorded April 15, 1956)
- Italy, Cetra LO 514 (3 LPs)
  - Reissued (1982) on Mahler: Symphonies as Italy, Fonit Cetra DOC 43 (8 LPs)

1981
The Westminster Choir Sings Familiar American and British Folk Songs
Westminster Choir, Flummerfelt
Westminster Recording Division WC 4 LP
- Reissued (1992) as Gothic Records 38130 CD, CAS

Menotti—Missa *"O Pulchritudo"*
Spoleto Festival Orchestra, Flummerfelt; Hong, Curry, di Paolo, Martinovich
Westminster Choir, Flummerfelt
(Recorded in 1981 at Spoleto Festival USA, Charleston, S.C.)
Westminster Recording Division WC 5 LP

Menotti—Missa *"O Pulchritudo"*
Spoleto Festival Orchestra, Badea; Bel Canto Chorus of Milwaukee
Westminster Choir, Flummerfelt
(Recorded in 1979 at Festival dei Due Mondi, Spoleto, Italy)
Italy, Fonit Cetra FDM 0001 (LP)

1983
Liszt—Faust Symphony with Symphonic Poem No. 3 "Les preludes"
Philadelphia Orchestra, Muti; Winberg
Men of the Westminster Choir, Flummerfelt
Angel DSB-3928 2 LPS
- Reissued (1991) as EMI Classics 49062 CD

Christmas with the Westminster Choir
New Jersey Symphony Orchestra, Flummerfelt
Westminster Choir, Flummerfelt
Beckwith, organ; Parker, piano
Book-of-the-Month Club, Inc. 71-6664 LPS
- Reissued (1992) as Gothic Records 47931 CD

Joseph G. Beck

1984
Barber—Anthony and Cleopatra, Op. 40
Spoleto Festival Orchestra, Badea; Hinds, Bunnell, Wells, Halfvarson
Westminster Choir, Flummerfelt
New World Records 322/24 (2 CDs)
  • Reissued (1991) as New World Records 322 (2 CDs)

1985
Beethoven—Missa Solemnis, Op. 123
New York Philharmonic, Mitropoulos; Steber, Tangeman, Smith-Spencer, Harrell
Westminster Choir, Williamson
(Recorded November 8, 1953)
Italy, Melodram 233 (2 LPs)

1986
Scriabin—Symphony No. 1
Philadelphia Orchestra, Muti; Toczyska, Myers
Westminster Symphonic Choir, Flummerfelt
(Recorded 1985)
Angel/EMI DS-38260 (LPS); 4DS-38260 CAS; CDC-47349 CD

Berlioz—Romeo and Juliet
Philadelphia Orchestra, Muti; Norman, Aler, Estes
Westminster Symphonic Choir, Flummerfelt
U.S.A., as Angel DSB-3997 (2 LPS), 4D2S-3997 (CS)
England, as EMI CDS 747437/38 (2 CDs)
  • Reissued (1995) as EMI 65576 (2 CDs)
  • Reissued (1998) on Berlioz: Roméo et Juliette and La Nuit d'été as EMI Classics 72640 (2 CDs)

130

1988

Mahler—Symphony No. 2
New York Philharmonic, Bernstein; Hendricks, Ludwig
Westminster Symphonic Choir, Flummerfelt
Deutsche Grammophon 23395 CD (2 CDs)

- Reissued (1991) on Mahler: 10 Symphonies as Deutsche Grammophon 435162 (CDs)
- Reissued (1995) excerpt on Mad About Angels as Deutsche Grammophon 2FM 449113 (CD)
- Reissued (1998) on Bernstein/Mahler: The Complete Symphonies and Orchestral Songs as Deutsche Grammophon 459080 (16 CDs)
- Reissued (1998) excerpts on Leonard Bernstein: Reaching for the Note as Deutsche Grammophon 459552 (2 CDs)

Beethoven—Symphony No. 9
Philadelphia Orchestra, Muti; Studer, Zeigler, Sieffert, Morris
Westminster Symphonic Choir, Flummerfelt
Angel/EMI 49493 CD, CAS

- Reissued (1998) on Beethoven: The Complete Symphonies and Selected Overtures, EMD/EMI Classics 72923 (6 CDs)
- Reissued (1999) as EMI/Seraphim 73284 CD

1989

Verdi—Te Deum
NBC Orchestra, Toscanini
Westminster Choir, Williamson
(Recorded Feb 12, 1945)
Melodram (Milano, Italy) CD

- Reissued (2000) with Verdi Requiem (LaScala Orchestra and Chorus) as IDI 345/6 CD

Verdi—Messa da Requiem
New York Philharmonic, Cantelli; Nelli, Turner, Tucker, Hines
Westminster Choir, Williamson
(Recorded February 6, 1955)
Italy, AS Disc AS 521 (CD; Allegro Imports, U.S. distributor)

1990

Favorite Hymns and Anthems
Westminster Choir, Flummerfelt; Lippincott, Arnatt
Gothic Records 49044 CD, CAS

- Reissued (1992) as Gothic Records 38130 CD

1992

Wagner—"Venusberg Lied" (from Tannhauser)
New York Philharmonic, Mehta
Westminster Symphonic Choir, Flummerfelt
(Recorded in 1989)
Sony Classical SK 45749 CD

O Magnum Mysterium
Westminster Choir, Flummerfelt
Parrella, organ
Chesky Records 83 CD, CAS
- Reissued (1995) excerpts on The Classical Collection as Chesky Classical 135

Menotti—Goya
Spoleto Festival Orchestra, Mercurio; Daner, Guzman, Hernandez, Bender, Senator, Wentzel
Westminster Choir, Flummerfelt
(Recorded in 1991)
Italy, Nuova Era 7060/61 (2 CDs)

Verdi—"Va pensiero sull'ali dorate" from Nabucco
The Philadelphia Orchestra and Riccardo Muti: In Celebration of His 20 Years in Philadelphia
Philadelphia Orchestra, Muti
Westminster Symphonic Choir, Flummerfelt
(Recorded February 10, 1989)
Philadelphia Orchestra POA92 (CD) [not commercial]

1993

Leoncavallo—Pagliacci
Philadelphia Orchestra, Muti; Pavarotti, Dessi, Pons, Coni, Gavazzi, Boyd, Newman, Philadelphia Boys Choir
Westminster Symphonic Choir, Flummerfelt
(Recorded February 1992)
Philips Classics 38132 CD

Puccini—Tosca
Philadelphia Orchestra, Muti; Vaness, Giacomini, Zancanaro, Philadelphia Boys Choir
Westminster Symphonic Choir, Flummerfelt
(Recorded in 1991 and 1992)
Philips Classics 434595-2 (2 CDs)

1994

Dvorak—Stabat Mater
New Jersey Symphony Orchestra, Macal; Erickson, Carlson, Aler, Cheek (Stabat Mater); Hemm (Biblical Songs)
with Biblical Songs, Op. 99/B 185
Westminster Symphonic Choir, Flummerfelt
Delos International 3161 (2 CDs)
- Reissued (1995) excerpts on Horizons: A Musical Journey as Delos International 3511 (CD)
- Reissued (1995) excerpt on Surround Spectacular: The Music, The Tests as Delos 3179 (2 CDs)
- Reissued (1997) excerpt on Visions of Heaven as Delos International 3227 (CD)

1995
Brahms—Requiem
New York Philharmonic, Masur; McNair, Hagegard
Westminster Symphonic Choir, Flummerfelt
Teldec 98413 CD

Like as a Hart: Psalms and Spiritual Songs
Westminster Choir, Flummerfelt
Parrella, organ
Chesky Records 138 CD

1996
Singing for Pleasure: The Westminster Choir Sings Brahms
Westminster Choir, Flummerfelt
Parker and Parrella, pianists
Delos International DE 3193 CD

Westminster Choir at the Spoleto Festival U.S.A.
Westminster Choir, Flummerfelt
Parker and Parrella, pianists
Gothic Records G49078 CD

Brahms—Schicksalslied, Op. 54
New York Philharmonic, Masur
Westminster Symphonic Choir, Flummerfelt
Symphonies No. 1-4, Overtures and Variations
Teldec 13565 (4 CDs)
 • Reissued (1998) as Teldec 13695 (CD)

Joseph G. Beck

1997
Heaven and Hell: Macal conducts Mussorgsky
"Dream of the Peasant Gritzko" (Night on Bald Mountain) et al
New Jersey Symphony Orchestra, Macal; Brainerd
Westminster Symphonic Choir, Flummerfelt
Delos International 3217 CD
- Reissued (1997) on Engineer's Choice 2 as Delos International 3512 (CD)

1998
Britten—War Requiem
New York Philharmonic Orchestra, Masur; Vaness, Hadley, Hampson
American Boy Choir, Litten
Westminster Symphonic Choir, Flummerfelt
(Recorded in 1997)
Teldec 17115 (2 CDs)

2000
Dvorak—Requiem and Symphony No. 9
New Jersey Symphony Orchestra, Macal; Krovytska, Hoffman, Aler, Belacek
Westminster Symphonic Choir, Flummerfelt
Delos International 3260 (2 CDs)

Bellini—"Ite Sul Colle, o Druidi" from Norma
Toscanini: His Romantic Rarities
NBC Symphony Orchestra, Toscanini; Mascona
Westminster Choir, Williamson
Italy, Iron Needle IN 1420 CD

Weill—Die Bürgschaft
Spoleto Festival Orchestra, Rudel; Panagulias, Thompson, Sorenson, Burchinal
Westminster Choir, Megill
(Recorded at the 1999 Spoleto Festival USA, Charleston, SC)
EMI Classics 56976 (2 CDs)

2001

Mahler—Symphony No. 8
The Mahler Broadcasts 1948-1982
New York Philharmonic Orchestra, Stokowski; Yeend, Graf, Alexander, Conley, Williams, Lipton, Bernhardt, London
Schola Cantorum, Ross
Public School No. 12 Boy's Choir, Covner
Westminster Choir, Williamson
(Recorded April 9, 1950)
Arkadia 78586 CD
New York Philharmonic Label 9801(12 CDs)
- Reissued (2001) as Arkadia 78586

Additional Resources

Bispham, David. A Quaker Singer's Recollections. New York: MacMillan Company, 1922.

Bristol, Lee Jr. Westminster Choir College: 'A College of Music to Sing About'. New York: Newcomen Society, 1965.

Robinson, Ray. John Finley Williamson: A Centennial Appreciation. Princeton, NJ: Prestige Publications, 1987.

Samuel, Christopher. "A History of Westminster Choir College." Westminster Choir College of Rider University Alumni Directory: 75 Magnificent Years. Purchase, NY: Bernard C. Harris Publishing, 2001.

Schisler, Charles Harvey. A History of Westminster Choir College, 1926-1973. Bloomington, IN: Indiana University, 1975.

Walter, Bruno. Theme and Variations: An Autobiorgaphy. New York: Alfred A. Knopf, 1959

Wehr, David A. John Finley Williamson (1887-1964): His Life and Contribution to Choral Music. Miami, FL: University of Miami, 1971.

Williamson, John Finley. "Choir Organization and Training." Papers and Proceedings of the Music Teachers National Association 1925. Hartford, CT: Music Teachers National Association, 1926. 226-30.

Winslow, Carlette Mueller. "Time to Build". Westminster Choir College Alumni Newsletter (December 1984): 1,4-5.

Witherspoon, Herbert. Singing. New York: DaCapo Press, 1980.

Printed in the United States
19404LVS00001B/118-171